PRAISE FOR
A Teacher's Guide to Flexible Grouping and Collaborative Learning

"The authors provide the most comprehensive guide to group learning that I have seen in my quarter century of teaching and researching grouping and talent development. The introductory sections reviewing relevant research and responding to common (and misguided) criticisms and myths of grouping are excellent and easily digestible, and the countless strategies and tips will prove useful for anyone working with K–12 students or supervising educators who do. This book should be required reading in all of our teacher preparation programs!"

—**Jonathan Plucker**, Julian C. Stanley Professor of Talent Development, Johns Hopkins Center for Talented Youth and School of Education

"An excellent read that both demystifies and clarifies what exactly is grouping and how it can be used as an effective method for instruction and assessment in the modern mixed-ability classroom. Dina Brulles and Karen Brown explain the benefits of teaching and learning through grouping in a clear and comprehensive manner. More importantly, they provide concrete and creative examples of best practices and instructional methods educators can use to address and respond to the diverse yet individual academic and socioemotional needs of *all* students. If your goal is to develop and deliver deeper, student-centered learning experiences that prompt deeper thinking and promote talent development, then this is the book you need to read!"

—**Erik M. Francis, M.Ed., M.S.**, professional education specialist at Maverik Education LLC and author of *Now That's a Good Question!*

"*A Teacher's Guide to Flexible Grouping and Collaborative Learning* provides the compelling *why* flexible grouping is essential for achieving equity in today's diverse classrooms, as well as detailed classroom scenarios and relatable real-world examples demonstrating *how* flexible grouping has been successfully implemented in elementary and secondary classrooms to support the unique needs of *each* student. The specific teaching and learning strategies and usable tools included provide *what* teachers and students need to accomplish truly personalized learning within today's classrooms."

—**Dr. Lauri B. Kirsch**, supervisor, K–12 gifted programs, Hillsborough County Public Schools, Tampa, FL

"One of the most challenging aspects of teaching in today's diverse classroom is the differentiated practice of effectively using flexible grouping and collaborative learning. Teaching and learning experts Brulles and Brown have aptly addressed these practices in this remarkably well-articulated text. Everything you need to know, understand, and be able to do are spelled out in a comprehensive manner. This step-by-step text gives you all the tools, directions, and methods for making flexible grouping and collaboration work in your classroom. This 'go-to' resource should be on every teacher's desk; studied, highlighted, tabbed, and applied!"

—**Richard M. Cash, Ed.D.**, author of *Advancing Differentiation: Thinking and Learning for the 21st Century*

"We know from research that collaboration can enhance learning; however, group work can be 'messy' at times. All too often, teachers avoid putting their students into groups because they think it wastes time or is just too difficult to manage. Brulles and Brown have written a book for teachers who are looking for more *flexibility* in how to form and manage groups for different purposes. They provide a plethora of learning activities and questioning strategies that are classroom tested and easily implemented to meet the needs of a range of learners—from ways to vary to the complexity of tasks to how to design engaging group projects. This book offers new ideas to novice and veteran teachers alike."

—**Karin Hess, Ed.D.**, researcher and author of *A Local Assessment Toolkit to Promote Deeper Learning: Transforming Research into Practice*

A TEACHER'S GUIDE TO
FLEXIBLE GROUPING AND
COLLABORATIVE LEARNING

FORM, MANAGE, ASSESS, AND DIFFERENTIATE IN GROUPS

DINA BRULLES, PH.D. | KAREN L. BROWN, M.ED.

free spirit
PUBLISHING®

Library of Congress Cataloging-in-Publication Data
Names: Brulles, Dina, author. | Brown, Karen L., 1960– author.
Title: A teacher's guide to flexible grouping and collaborative learning : form, manage, assess, and differentiate in groups / Dina Brulles and Karen L. Brown.
Description: Minneapolis, MN : Free Spirit Publishing, 2018. | Includes bibliographical references and index.
Identifiers: LCCN 2017035588 (print) | LCCN 2017056968 (ebook) | ISBN 9781631982842 (Web PDF) | ISBN 9781631982859 (ePub) | ISBN 9781631982835 (paperback) | ISBN 1631982834 (paperback)
Subjects: LCSH: Group work in education. | Group work in education—Evaluation. | BISAC: EDUCATION / Teaching Methods & Materials / General.
Classification: LCC LB1032 (ebook) | LCC LB1032 .B79 2018 (print) | DDC 371.3/6—dc23
LC record available at https://lccn.loc.gov/2017035588

Free Spirit Publishing does not have control over or assume responsibility for author or third-party websites and their content. At the time of this book's publication, all facts and figures cited within are the most current available. All telephone numbers, addresses, and website URLs are accurate and active; all publications, organizations, websites, and other resources exist as described in this book; and all have been verified as of November 2017. If you find an error or believe that a resource listed here is not as described, please contact Free Spirit Publishing. Parents, teachers, and other adults: We strongly urge you to monitor children's use of the internet.

All details, quotes, and names of teachers and students in this book have been changed to protect privacy, except for those, where noted, that were shared with permission.

Cover and book design by Shannon Pourciau
Edited by Meg Bratsch

10 9 8 7 6 5 4 3 2 1
Printed in the United States of America

Free Spirit Publishing Inc.
6325 Sandburg Road, Suite 100
Minneapolis, MN 55427-3674
(612) 338-2068
help4kids@freespirit.com
www.freespirit.com

DEDICATION

We dedicate this book to:

Susan Winebrenner, whose longstanding work has been a foundation in our field and for teachers throughout the world in their efforts to differentiate curriculum and instruction for all learners.

Our husbands, Dr. Mark Joraanstad and Daniel Brown, for their continual support and patience during the writing process of the book and the countless hours we spend working with and supporting teachers.

ACKNOWLEDGMENTS

To Dr. Karen Rogers, whose work on student grouping methods inspired and guided us in writing this book.

To Meg Bratsch, whose exceptional editing skills turned our ideas into a reality that will support teachers in their efforts to creatively teach students in flexible learning groups.

To Judy Galbraith, for her vision in creating outstanding support materials to help all children learn, and to the Free Spirit Publishing staff who continue to provide invaluable resources to educators and parents.

To the gifted teachers in Paradise Valley Unified School District in Arizona, whose extraordinary teaching and passion for learning have provided us countless opportunities to learn alongside them.

Contents

PART ONE: Rationale and Methods for Grouping Students in Mixed-Ability Classrooms 11

PART TWO: Instructional Strategies for Flexible Learning Groups 101

List of Figures

List of Figures, continued

List of Reproducible Forms

See page 182 for a link to download customizable digital versions of all reproducible forms.

Foreword by Karen B. Rogers

When asked to write a foreword for this book, I wondered if there was anything "new under the sun" that Dina Brulles and Karen Brown could write about grouping students to address their learning needs. Hadn't we hashed and rehashed the multiple ways in which students can be grouped to differentiate for their needs for at least the past 100 years, dating from the work of Lewis Terman and Lulu Stedman to the research synthesis that James and Chen-Lin Kulik and I have done? The research on why we need to group, and what forms that grouping can take, is long and plentiful. But then I began reading this remarkably in-depth and teacher-centered book on flexible grouping. What immediately struck me was that this was not a rehash at all, but a powerful new guide in and of itself!

And what is it that makes this book so powerful? First, the book spends its first few chapters explaining *in classroom terms* what grouping might look like. This offers teachers who are reading the book a chance to put themselves into an effectively grouped classroom in which they have a structure and control over how learning will take place for every learner in that setting. As these chapters progress, teachers are not judged if they are not currently grouping; the research is not thrown at them to point out what students are missing. A teacher's satisfaction in seeing students' learning becomes the rationale for making the effort to group. Right up there in these first chapters are the ways teachers will be able to look at these changes in learning. Of all the very specific and helpful chapters, chapter 3 is my favorite in part one of the book. The many options teachers have for preassessing what students already know, for formatively assessing how students' learning (and their instruction) is going, and for summative assessments truly open up the choices teachers have. The advice on how to manage time spent assessing and grading is golden. It is possible for teachers to enjoy providing differentiated instruction and to enjoy watching the learning that is taking place without being burdened by many more hours grading student work.

Second, the book lays out the small but important steps in creating grouping structures. Reading the frequent classroom scenarios that point out the strengths as well as the issues of various grouping strategies made me (and I hope other readers of this book) feel like I was in the classroom and could do this without creating chaos in terms of time off task and distracting noise. What became clear was that Brulles and Brown could have titled their book *Chaos in the Classroom—Not Here and Not Today!* It is helpful, too, that the authors spent much time on how teachers can make these groups work and stay on task. Behavior management is an underlying strength of the book. Again, the scenarios are detailed enough to enable the reader to see what is described as really happening in a classroom today. The writing is clear and direct in the directions it provides for teachers to make this happen in their own classrooms.

And third, the book's final several chapters get right down to the nitty-gritty of what the teacher is to do when students have been appropriately grouped. In this latter part of the book, I kept asking myself, where was this book in my preservice teacher training in California, where, at the time, we were required to group for specific subject instruction by reading ability and performance? My favorite chapter in part two of the book is chapter 6, with chapter 5 coming in a close second. Both chapters are chock-full of very specific activities and experiences that teachers can easily carry out. The message seems to be that the teacher will not be left without an adequate structure and plan for what to do for each of the multiple groups found in a single classroom. The strategies—some new, some relabeled—are the most complete compendium I have seen about what teachers can do. Notice, I did not say "should" do. Teachers get choices, just as they will provide choices to their students. This portion of the book empowers teachers to take a chance of changing a few years-old or age-old pedagogies for the purpose of teaching and assessing *for* learning.

In reflecting on the overall messages of this book, it seems as if Brulles and Brown have moved us away from allowing local, subject, and national curriculum standards to restrict the content teachers will choose to teach. The authors provide teachers with myriad ways to differentiate their chosen content rather than the standards themselves. I think this eases the burden for teachers and puts some joy and creativity back into their teaching. It bodes well for keeping their students motivated and engaged in their learning and ensuring that optimal learning is happening for all students in a classroom.

This book will be a gift to every school district or school in the country that is serious about professional learning for teachers. I know teachers will find this a gift, if in no other form than they will have many new and exciting ways to go about instructing and assessing their learners. It *almost* makes me want to go back into the classroom to try out every single one of these strategies. Brava!

Karen B. Rogers, Professor Emerita, Gifted Studies
University of St. Thomas, College of Education, Leadership, and Counseling
Minneapolis, Minnesota

Introduction

"If committed educators could be easily trained to implement a low-cost intervention that boasted consistent learning gains for all students, headlines would herald the discovery of the educational holy grail. That low-cost intervention is here and readily available. It's called ability grouping."

—*Paula Olszewski-Kubilius, director,*
Center for Talent Development at Northwestern University

Educational trends and initiatives come and go, policies and mandates get updated, and standards and assessments are continually revised. Little stays the same in the world of education; we are constantly learning and evolving. However, for a variety of reasons, including some misperceptions, controversy over the practice of ability grouping remains prevalent throughout these changes. Much of this controversy involves broad generalizations people make about grouping students. In this book, we attempt to dispel the myths surrounding ability grouping while sharing teaching practices that are effective in a variety of grouping models.

It is important to note that we are not advocating tracking. Rather, we are providing teachers with practical methods for determining classroom compositions, forming and managing flexible learning groups, designing tiered assignments, and teaching in a variety of settings where students are purposefully grouped. In brief, this book is an educator's guide for learning how to recognize and respond to students' diverse learning needs. To this end, we share methods for grouping students for specific content and suggestions for structuring the classroom to accommodate the needs of a range of students. We also examine methods for using achievement data to inform grouping, monitor students' progress, and document achievement gains.

Equity vs. Equality

Let's begin by considering the issue of "equity" in our schools. We often hear this as the reason schools choose not to group students according to learning needs. The rationale is that all students, not just certain groups, should have equal access to resources. In this section, we will discuss how incorporating grouping practices can, in fact, ensure equitable access for all students based on learning needs.

Much confusion exists surrounding the differences between equity and equality, especially involving students of special populations. Here are some key distinctions:

Equality means the exact *same* elements exist for all students, regardless of experiences or needs: the same placement, same curriculum, same expectations, same funding, and same level of instruction.

Equity means that treatment, access, learning, and resources are considered for all students based on what students need to achieve and succeed at their own levels, which are determined by their unique experiences and needs.

1

We need to use an *equity* lens to make educational decisions; this practice enables us to create the necessary changes to meet our goals for every student. If we are instead seeking equality for all students, then we must ask ourselves if we are, in fact, creating barriers for some students by not providing equitable opportunities for them to achieve at their highest possible levels. Without purposefully grouping students, it is extremely difficult to provide these opportunities and make instructional decisions that meet the needs of all students.

Goals of Education Equity:[1]

- High achievement and positive outcomes for *all* students

- Equitable access and inclusion

- Equitable treatment

- Equitable resource distribution

- Equitable opportunity to learn

- Shared accountability

When schools consciously plan for equitable measures, they can more easily demonstrate students' achievement gains, since they are routinely collecting and analyzing achievement data to form flexible learning groups and document student growth in the various groups. In turn, these groups require equitable distribution of resources so that all students receive equal opportunities to learn. Ultimately, the process becomes a shared responsibility of schools and teachers that leads to equitable treatment, access, and inclusion for all.

The Objectives of This Book

Specifically, this book will guide teachers in how to implement the following twelve objectives:

1. *Develop* flexible learning groups.

2. *Use* data to form flexible groups.

3. *Plan* lessons for flexible groups in a mixed-ability classroom.

4. *Assign* purposeful and individualized classwork and homework.

5. *Know* your efforts are working.

6. *Design* a daily schedule to accommodate project-based learning.

7. *Assess* and grade collaborative work.

8. *Work* with digital natives (even if you are a digital immigrant).

9. *Match* instructional strategies to students' social and emotional characteristics and academic needs.

10. *Engage* nonperforming learners.

11. *Support* a personalized learning environment.

12. *Build* a communication network with parents.

These twelve objectives are described in detail throughout this book. We present an overview of each objective in this section. Due to the various grouping

---

1. IDRA. (March 31, 2006). "Six Goals of Educational Equity." idra.org/equity-assistance-center/six-goals-of-education-equity.

formats implemented in schools, you will find these objectives are applicable in several ways. Your current situation, your plans to implement change, your school's structures and initiatives, and your programming and instructional goals will determine which objectives you implement initially and which you may consider for later implementation.

Objective 1. Develop flexible learning groups. Flexible grouping means that the groups continually change depending on the lesson and the topics involved. Students can be flexibly grouped according to:

- learning objectives
- student interests
- learning preferences
- products or projects
- achievement levels
- formative assessments and pretest results

In chapter 1, we describe methods for forming flexible learning groups.

Objective 2. Use data to form flexible groups. Educators today have more access to achievement data than ever before. Schools routinely provide benchmark assessments and analyze data during professional learning communities (PLCs) and within Response to Intervention (RTI) structures. In chapter 3, you will learn methods for using the following data to form flexible groups within a grade level, across grade levels, or within a class:

- formal and informal assessments
- benchmark assessments
- PLC data
- RTI structures

Objective 3. Plan lessons for flexible groups in a mixed-ability classroom. In all school-based learning environments—including classrooms, grade levels, or schools that use "fixed" learning groups—most teachers find they have a range of abilities in their classes. Meeting the diverse needs in your classes requires you to develop tiered learning activities appropriate for your students' different learning levels. In chapter 5, we demonstrate how to create lessons tiered to knowledge levels and provide suggestions for tiering activities using student choice menus.

Objective 4. Assign purposeful and individualized classwork and homework. To assign appropriately leveled learning activities to groups of students, teachers need to determine how they will assess those learning levels. They must also recognize that even with students of similar ability levels, they'll need to modify lessons for exceptional individual needs or interests. In this book, we also describe methods for designing homework that supports or extends students' differentiated group learning activities.

Objective 5. Know your efforts are working. In today's era of accountability, teachers are expected to document individual student growth. This requirement may concern you when providing opportunities for differentiated learning activities for your students. You may wonder: "How do I really know my efforts are working when students are all working on different projects?" "How can I accurately measure student achievement for the different learning groups in my class?" "How do I document progress?" and "How does this documentation inform my instruction?" We address these questions specifically in chapter 3, and throughout the book, within the frameworks of grouping compositions, instructional strategies, and progress monitoring.

Objective 6. Design a daily schedule to accommodate project-based learning. You will notice that many of the grouping strategies in this book follow a project-based learning (PBL) format. PBL is a teaching method in which students gain knowledge and skills by working for an extended period to investigate and respond to an authentic, engaging, and complex question, problem, or challenge. This format integrates subjects, which many students enjoy and thrive on, especially those with high ability. PBL also helps prepare students for performance-based assessments. In chapter 5, we demonstrate methods that allow teachers to incorporate PBL format needs and time requirements.

Objective 7. Assess and grade collaborative work. Twenty-first century skills rely on collaborative learning, and assessing growth and assigning grades looks different when students collaborate on projects in groups. We need to teach students how to collaborate so there is accountability for everyone. Throughout the book, you will learn methods for grading and structuring assignments that encourage student collaboration and accountability.

Objective 8. Work with digital natives (even if you are a digital immigrant). As a teacher today, you are surrounded by ubiquitous technology with endless resources at your fingertips. Technology integration can greatly ease your ability to manage varied learning groups. Numerous methods are described in chapter 7, "Differentiating Digitally in Groups." By introducing educational apps and making digital resources available to your students, you provide additional opportunities for them to become involved in directing their own learning.

Objective 9. Match instructional strategies to students' social and emotional characteristics and academic needs. When students feel understood and accepted by teachers, they are more likely to take academic risks. Learning how to align specific teaching strategies to students' learning traits can solve many learning challenges for students and instructional challenges for teachers. This alignment demonstrates respect for students' differences and sets the stage for real learning to occur.

Objective 10. Engage nonperforming learners. Teachers create lessons that engage and motivate students by building on their strengths and developing their interests. We have all witnessed underachieving and nonperforming students in our classes. The easiest way to address these learners is to ask yourself, "Why are they not achieving?" Often, the answer is an easy one: they are not engaged or motivated by the lesson or topic. This is particularly evident with high-ability students, who commonly have their own ideas they would rather pursue. Strategies described throughout this book allow students to build on their interests and develop their areas of strength through the content addressed in the lessons and standards.

Objective 11. Support a personalized learning environment. Differentiation is not about creating an individualized program for every student, but rather a personalized learning environment. Personalized learning is everywhere in our ever-changing world of education. The potential in personalized learning is immense; educators see it as a way to address the learning needs of a student population that grows more diverse every day. In this book, we will look at the definition of personalized learning and its impact on students, particularly in groups, in today's technology-infused classrooms.

Objective 12. Build a communication network with parents. Regular parent communication is critical when using flexible grouping structures. Parents need information about how you are forming/reforming student learning groups and how curriculum and instruction differ between the groups. Building a communication network with your parents eases the practice and keeps parents informed of their children's progress, including information about advanced academic progress as well as the benefits of productive struggle.

Flexible Grouping: Confronting the Criticism and Overcoming the Obstacles

Despite ongoing educational reforms, improved standards, new testing methods, data-based decision-making in schools, and instructional innovations, the debate over ability grouping has continued over several decades. In a 1996 article, "The Elephant in the Classroom," authors Ellis Page and Timothy Keith confront the criticism that ability grouping is "harmful to minority students."[2] Opponents of purposeful ability grouping commonly cite that it has negative achievement effects for students in diverse populations and of low socioeconomic status. And yet, in studying the effects of ability grouping on low-ability black and Hispanic students, Page and Keith's research yielded data showing "no substantive positive or negative effect on achievement for these groups." In their study, homogenous grouping for these students was neither helpful nor harmful. However, homogenous groups of high-ability students clearly *did* yield positive effects on achievement.

Likewise, researchers Chen-Lin Kulik and James Kulik studied the achievement of students of different ability levels in schools that ability grouped compared with those that did not. Over the years, their research consistently documented substantive growth for students of high ability when grouped together.[3] Other researchers over the past two decades have noted moderate to significant growth for all groups of students when purposefully grouped in classrooms. According to a 2010 meta-analysis, "Students who were grouped by ability within a class for reading were able to make up to an additional half of a year's growth in reading."[4]

In short, flexible ability grouping has been proven to work when used appropriately. This is especially true now; we have infinitely more tools and resources needed to make informed decisions when grouping students.

---

2. Page, E., and Keith, T. (1996). "The Elephant in the Classroom: Ability Grouping and the Gifted." In *Intellectual Talent* edited by C. P. Benbow and D. J. Lubinski (Baltimore, MD: Johns Hopkins University Press).

3. Kulik, C. C., and Kulik, J. A. (1982). "Effects of Ability Grouping on Secondary School Students: A Meta-Analysis of Evaluation Findings." *American Educational Research Journal,* 19(3), 415–428; Kulik, J. A., and Kulik, C. C. (1987). "Effects of Ability Grouping on Student Achievement." *Equity & Excellence in Education,* 23(1–2), 22–30; Kulik, J. A., and Kulik, C. C. (1992). "Meta-Analytic Findings on Grouping Programs." *Gifted Child Quarterly* 36(2), 73–77.

4. Puzio, K., and Colby, G. T. (March 2010). "The Effects of Within-Class Grouping on Reading Achievement: A MetaAnalytic Synthesis." Paper presented at the annual meeting of the Society for Research on Educational Effectiveness (SREE), Washington, DC.

Given the controversy surrounding the practices of grouping students for instructional purposes, it is important to address the prevailing myths that contribute to misunderstandings of the practice.

Myth 1. Groupings are usually permanent. When used properly, ability grouping allows for flexibility, letting students move in and out of groups according to learning needs and interests. For example, some schools group for certain content areas. We suggest forming learning groups using diagnostic tests given monthly or quarterly throughout the year depending on the course content. Students are then regrouped according to the pretest (diagnostic testing) results for that specific content. Other schools group for specialized programming, such as with special education classes, English language learning (ELL) instruction, and Honors classes. These groupings usually change as students' learning needs change.

Myth 2. All grouping, including flexible grouping, is tracking. Grouping students together is different than tracking. In tracking scenarios, the groups are usually fixed, meaning they stay the same year after year. In tracking systems, curriculum is typically based on the achievement levels of the students in each track. In contrast, teachers flexibly group students to modify or extend grade-level standards according to the students' needs and abilities. The classroom compositions change frequently, sometimes for reasons not specifically related to achievement levels.

Myth 3. Groupings are based only on achievement levels. Teachers can group students within the class for various purposes, such as interests, project formats, lesson design, skills, and so on. Students can also self-select groups for certain projects. Varying the criteria for forming flexible learning groups can help engage and motivate students. They have opportunities to work with others who have similar interests, learning styles, or project goals.

Myth 4. Groupings only benefit high-ability and high-achieving students. For decades, schools have grouped students for special education services according to need. A teacher who has specialized training in an area teaches a particular group of students. In many states, a similar process is in place for teaching ELL students. Grouping these students for specific content instruction allows teachers to focus on the students' learning needs, which increases the effectiveness of teachers' instruction. These students can make greater gains academically with these systems in place. The same holds true for students of high ability or high achievement. Creating flexible groups for different purposes can address *all* students' learning needs.

Myth 5. Grouping students eliminates the need to differentiate instruction. Regardless of the way students are grouped or placed into classes, all classrooms require teachers to differentiate instruction. Even within homogenous classes of special education students, gifted students, or ELL students, there will be a wide range of learning needs. As individuals with varying experiences and strengths, all students—whether identified for a particular classification or not—need teachers who understand and respond to their learning needs. Therefore, grouping does not minimize the need for differentiated instruction.

Myth 6. Grouping discriminates against minority populations. Teachers often make assumptions about what students know and what they are capable of learning. For example, students of diversity, most commonly those who are black and

Hispanic, are widely underrepresented in programs for advanced learners. They are less likely to be identified as gifted or even nominated for testing. Yet, these students are as highly capable as any other student. When forming flexible ability groups, you analyze achievement data and determine interests within the confines of the curriculum being studied. This process requires you to know your students, their interests, what they know, and where they need help. Assumptions of what students can and cannot do are not valid reasons to restrict their growth, especially those who go largely unrecognized due to race, culture, language status, or socioeconomic status.

About This Book

In this book, we lead you through the process of teaching in flexibly grouped classrooms by first developing an understanding of grouping for effective instruction. We then discuss methods for forming and managing grouped classrooms. This leads us to instructional practices and support, lesson design, and the purpose and use of assessments in ability-grouped classes.

In our practice, we have found many teachers who want to incorporate flexible grouping practices into their routines that allow for targeted instruction. However, few teachers have the training or support to implement, manage, and document the effectiveness of groups. This book discusses best instructional practices and presents them in the context of teaching flexible learning groups within a classroom, grade level, or school. Part one of the book discusses why and how to group students in mixed-ability classrooms, and part two describes instructional methods for teaching in classes that flexibly group students.

This book is intended for teachers, school administrators, instructional coaches, and anyone involved in determining class placements or providing professional development. The purpose is twofold: The first is to guide school staff in determining appropriate classroom grouping. The second is to introduce methods for managing and effectively teaching to the needs of students with varying abilities and achievement levels, readiness, and interests.

With growing emphasis on creativity, critical thinking, and collaboration, schools are seeking methods that recognize and acknowledge students' diverse learning needs. Schools must modify curriculum and instruction accordingly to ensure that all students are appropriately engaged and challenged in meaningful learning activities. Flexible grouping methods, as detailed in this book, set the framework for such activities to occur.

Throughout the book, in the Classroom Scenarios and elsewhere, you will read about actual teachers in real classrooms. These teachers face the day-to-day challenges that every teacher deals with in a mixed-ability learning environment. They share their experiences, lessons, and strategies for supporting learners in groups. We hope these scenarios will show you firsthand how flexible grouping and collaborative learning opportunities can be used effectively in today's classrooms.

Using This Book

This book can be used to guide study sessions extended over a period of time, such as in professional learning communities (PLCs), after-school workshops, full-day in-service trainings, staff meetings, and numerous other formats. The first four chapters highlight ways to structure and manage the groups, establish routines, assess progress, communicate with parents, and create ongoing support systems. The final three chapters describe instructional strategies to use when incorporating flexible grouping. These strategies are useful for all learning groups, including those with learning struggles, advanced learners, English language learners, and so on. Readers will be guided in scaffolding instruction, incorporating depth of complexity, project-based learning, questioning strategies, and numerous other methods for meeting all students' learning needs when placed in flexible learning groups.

We recommend that you work through the book in the order the chapters are presented. This will help you develop an understanding of how to form your flexible learning groups and will increase the effectiveness of the strategies presented in part two. That said, you might wish to move back and forth through parts one and two to begin practicing and implementing the instructional strategies while you learn about the grouping structures.

Our goal is to provide you with a roadmap showing how to best challenge and engage all your students, every day, and in every subject. We describe a process and provide suggestions for how you can accomplish these goals; just remember, the process takes time. We encourage you to attempt one or two practices at a time, preferably with other interested colleagues. When you're comfortable with one strategy, identify another, and so on.

In **chapter 1,** we respond to the commonly asked question, "Why should we flexibly group students?" We describe popular models for ability grouping and discuss how these models can effectively serve all students. We discuss various methods for grouping students and creating effective classroom compositions using the cluster-grouping model as an example. We also address the controversies surrounding ability grouping from a practitioner's perspective. The chapter provides an overview of the diverse learning needs of our students; their characteristics, behavioral traits, and learning needs; and how these needs can be met using flexible ability grouping.

Chapter 2 describes methods for establishing structure in grouped classrooms and what a mixed-ability classroom looks like when students are flexibly grouped for specific learning objectives. It shows you how to structure and manage a class so that small, flexible groups can work on different but related lessons at the same time. The chapter discusses why training teachers to successfully manage student groups with multiple learning levels in one classroom is essential. The range of students' abilities demands that instruction occur at multiple challenge levels. Chapter 2 will also show you how to manage the different groups and the importance of designing differentiated lessons that follow a similar pace.

In **chapter 3**, we share information for both teachers and administrators on methods for collecting and analyzing data to gauge success in ability grouping. These methods are critical due to current changes in the ways students are assessed and teachers are evaluated. Assessment and evaluation are now based on individual student growth, which requires schools to adopt new methods for showing and documenting growth, especially when students are working below or above grade level.

While assessment is woven into every chapter pertaining to classroom instruction, chapter 3 discusses how to obtain and document ongoing achievement at all levels: in the classroom, throughout a school, and throughout the school district. We share methods for analyzing student achievement and progress daily, monthly, and yearly using formal and informal methods, formative and summative assessments, data at the school and state levels, benchmark assessments, and more. Also included are methods for grading students who are working on accelerated and/or differentiated schoolwork and how to create forms that document progress. Finally, we recommend several parent reporting methods and forms that document academic growth. At the end of the relevant chapters throughout the book, we provide you with documentation forms you can use or modify for your purposes.

We recognize that teachers need ongoing professional development to successfully teach in a mixed-ability classroom. In **chapter 4,** we describe methods for supporting teachers in using the strategies discussed throughout the book. Whether in a district or a single school, you will gain ideas for planning teacher workshops, peer coaching, PLC meetings, and more. We also discuss methods for accessing and sharing resources. Through examples from classroom teachers, we demonstrate how you can build a digital repository

> We encourage you to attempt one or two practices at a time, preferably with other interested colleagues. When you're comfortable with one strategy, identify another, and so on.

of differentiated lessons, curriculum, assessment data, and training tools such as videos, presentations, blogs, and online workshops. Lastly, we offer methods that school administrators can use to provide ongoing support for teachers.

Beginning part two, **chapter 5** addresses foundational instructional strategies. These strategies create structures for differentiated learning with an emphasis on grouping. They provide an overarching framework for addressing different groups' challenge levels. The strategies will help you extend learning for students who have mastered content prior to instruction or can master content more quickly than the rest of the class. These fundamental strategies are essential for managing flexible ability groups. You will learn how to implement the strategies so they are ongoing and can extend over a long period of time.

In **chapter 6,** we share strategies for forming flexible learning groups and creating differentiated lessons for these groups that add depth and complexity throughout the school day. The differentiation strategies in this chapter are designed for varied levels of learning groups, including groups of students struggling to master content, and can be incorporated into various subject areas. They take little preparation time and are easy to incorporate into daily instruction. These strategies provide depth and complexity, appeal to students' varying interests and learning styles, and incorporate critical thinking.

Chapter 7 provides methods for differentiating instruction digitally. Teachers today have access to a multitude of resources that open up a wealth of opportunities. In this chapter, we show teachers how to make use of digital tools and apps that engage and challenge students in learning groups. By sharing lesson samples from teachers we've worked with, we demonstrate how teachers can access these resources and incorporate them into their standard curriculum and grouping formats.

Lastly, the **digital content** accompanying this book includes:

- customizable versions of all the reproducible forms
- a PDF presentation for use in professional development

To download these materials, see page 182 for instructions.

A free downloadable **PLC/Book Study Guide** for use in PLCs and book study groups is also available at freespirit.com/PLC.

This book is designed to walk you through the process of flexibly grouping students with a clear purpose in mind. However, that is not the only goal. What occurs daily in your classroom is the critical factor in effective grouping practices. Our goal is for you to learn new methods and strategies not only for forming learning groups, but also for being a highly effective teacher to all students in those groups.

We'd love to hear how this book has helped you in your grouping and teaching endeavors. If you have stories or questions for us, you can reach us through our publisher at help4kids@freespirit.com or visit our website: giftededucationconsultants.com.

Dina Brulles and Karen Brown

PART ONE

Rationale and Methods
for Grouping Students in
Mixed-Ability Classrooms

CHAPTER 1
Why Flexibly Group Your Students?

GUIDING QUESTIONS:
- Why should we flexibly group?
- What are the various types of grouping methods and their benefits?
- What are some examples of effective ability grouping models that employ flexible learning groups?

This chapter provides an overview of flexible grouping strategies and discusses how these strategies can effectively serve all students. It also provides an overview of students' learning needs, which take into consideration their varied characteristics and behavioral traits. We demonstrate how these learning needs can be addressed using flexible grouping. We briefly describe the instructional benefits and differences within several grouping strategies, with a special focus on two models: cluster grouping and content replacement. In later chapters, we will discuss instructional strategies that align well within the various models described here.

Purposeful grouping enables all students at all instructional levels to be challenged and to advance academically. Grouping methods foster supportive school environments characterized by respect for what each student brings to our classes. In flexible grouping models, students work with peers who learn at similar rates, have similar interests, or share similar strengths and/or areas of concern.

The three main questions teachers ask when considering grouping students are:

1. How do we form groups?
2. What do we do once students are grouped?
3. How do we know the groups are working?

These three questions will be introduced in this chapter and addressed extensively throughout the book.

Flexible Grouping

"Groupings allow students to engage and work with both similar and dissimilar peers depending on the project and the purpose of the lesson."—*NAGC position paper, 2015*

Flexible grouping promotes high levels of achievement for all students and teachers use ongoing assessments to identify their students' challenge levels. Understanding and addressing students' challenge levels helps students achieve at high levels, which can result in shrinking excellence gaps.[1]

---

1. Plucker, J. A., and Peters, S. J. (2016). *Excellence Gaps in Education: Expanding Opportunities for Talented Students.* Cambridge, MA: Harvard Education Press.

Dr. Karen Rogers identifies two broad categories of grouping students: small groups and whole class. She describes small groups as including dyads (two students), clusters (five to eight students within a class), enrichment groups (eight to twelve students in a pullout class), and regroupings of students based on performance in specific subject areas.[2] Modifying and expanding upon Dr. Rogers's work, the following represents several grouping methods and structures.

SMALL-GROUP METHODS: FLEXIBLE GROUPS

Note: While most small groups are flexible groups, not all are. This list is simply a way to think about grouping, knowing there are exceptions.

- Pullout groups, often used for content replacement
- Within-class groups based on ability and/or achievement
- Regrouping for specific subjects based on ability and/or achievement
- Cooperative learning groups
- Cross-grade grouping by achievement levels

The students served within these small groups are typically homogeneous and have similar levels of intellect. However, achievement and/or ability levels are not the only criteria used to form small groups. Students' interests and learning styles, and the type of project can also determine the formation of these small groups. "Flexible ability grouping allows schools to match a student's readiness with instruction, delivering the right content to the right student at the right pace and at the right time."[3]

WHOLE-CLASS GROUPING METHODS: FIXED GROUPS

Note: While the following methods represent fixed grouping, all of them (except for tracking) also include opportunities for flexible grouping *within* the fixed-group placements.

- Tracking
- Like-ability cooperative grouping
- Special schools for students with special needs
- Self-contained programs
- School-within-a-school
- Cluster grouping
- Untracked whole-class instruction

These whole-group methods are typically formed based on achievement or ability testing data. While the groups typically remain the same for the entire school year (hence, "fixed"), most of these methods allow for the regrouping of students each year to reflect students' needs.

Of the fixed groups listed above, the first five represent *homogenous* groupings: tracking, like-ability cooperative groupings, special schools for students with special

2. Rogers, K. B. (2002). *Re-Forming Gifted Education: Matching the Program to the Child.* Scottsdale, AZ: Great Potential Press.
3. Rogers (2002).

needs,[4] self-contained programs, and a school-within-a-school. This means that the students have been placed in the classes based on specific criteria, most commonly achievement and/or ability levels. Cluster grouping and untracked whole-class instruction represent *heterogeneous* groupings. Unlike with the first group noted on the list, classroom compositions for these latter two grouping methods change each year.

TWO MAIN VARIATIONS OF FLEXIBLE GROUPS

As we just discussed, two main flexible small grouping variations include *regrouping for specific instruction* and *within-class groupings*. Some teachers rely solely on regrouping for specific instruction and some incorporate both grouping methods for more targeted instruction.

Regrouping for Specific Instruction

When regrouping for a particular subject, all teachers in the grade level must teach the same subject at the same time. Teachers use formative and summative achievement data to assign students to daily flexible learning groups for a specific subject area, usually math and/or reading. Typically, a teacher experienced in working with advanced students takes the highest group, a teacher with training in special education may take struggling learners, and a teacher experienced with ELL students may take that group. Some teachers using this practice reassess and regroup periodically, for instance, monthly or quarterly according to the content being taught and the needs of the students.

Within-Class Groupings

This method is the most common grouping method in most classes. Within-class groupings can (and should) occur in *both* small-group and whole-class grouping methods. The teacher creates flexible learning groups within the class based on readiness, interests, learning preferences, and so on. Data from preassessments, students' interests and goals, and lesson objectives can help determine the groupings. The teacher then differentiates the learning activities according to these groups' needs.

The reproducible chart on pages 27–28 provides a quick reference of many of the grouping terms and formats just discussed.

REQUIREMENTS AND BENEFITS OF ALL FLEXIBLE GROUPING MODELS

Regardless of the grouping structure in place, all students have the right to appropriately challenging curriculum and an environment that encourages divergent thinking and learning time with peers. For this to occur, certain elements must be in place: *continual assessment, targeted instruction, focus on specific learning objectives, learner confidence,* and *differentiated instruction.*

Following are more details on each of the five beneficial required elements for effective flexible grouping.

Ongoing formative assessment. Continual assessment is required to form flexible groups. Data collected to form the flexible groups provides documentation of

---

4. For the purpose of this book, "students with special needs" refers to students who are identified as either qualifying for special education or gifted education, are ELL, are former ELL, are culturally diverse, or are living in poverty.

progress, which is especially useful for gifted students working beyond grade level. Continual assessment relies on both formal and informal assessment data to form and reform flexible learning groups according to what students already know about the content that is to be taught. When teachers use different methods for ongoing assessment, they are constantly monitoring student achievement and identifying areas that need additional support or intervention.

Targeted instruction. Assessment results provide evidence of mastery and needs, informing teachers what students already know and what they need to know. When students are flexibly grouped based on achievement data, teachers can more purposefully target their instruction to the specific needs of the group.

Focus on specific learning objectives. Continual assessment and targeted instruction keeps our focus on the specific objectives of the lesson. Even though all students in the class are learning the same topics, the flexible groups may have different objectives. The objectives created for each group depend on the specific needs of each group.

Learner confidence. When students are flexibly grouped with like peers, the level of academic risk-taking increases significantly. The group becomes a safe place to "push the learning envelope." Confidence levels build when students work on challenging learning goals. The data collected helps direct teachers in designing learning opportunities that build on students' readiness levels and interests.

Differentiated curriculum and instruction. When students are purposely grouped according to a targeted need, teachers can more readily structure their curriculum and instruction across a grade level or within a class. Having this documentation justifies the need for differentiated instruction based on the students' needs.

The benefits of grouping strategies vary depending on the methods employed given the needs of the situation. Clearly, the skill and training of the teachers greatly impacts the benefits, as is the case with all instruction. For this reason, we strongly advocate for ongoing training, such as that described in chapter 4.

Understanding Learning Behaviors

Though ability levels manifest differently in children, some students do share common behavioral traits, such as tendencies toward intensities, perfectionism, and hypersensitivity. Some children overachieve, some may underachieve, and some may be unmotivated or disengaged from classroom instruction. Idiosyncrasies typical of different populations can interfere with learning and academic achievement if teachers are unaware of the source. Thus, it is critical that teachers with students with special needs participate in ongoing training to understand their students' behaviors and learning needs, so they can group and instruct students effectively.

All students are more likely to seek challenging work and take academic risks when they feel accepted by peers and understood by their teachers. Learning alongside students who share similar affective concerns and academic abilities provides the setting many students need to challenge themselves. Teachers who understand these learning behaviors can better create the environment and flexible learning groups their students need to thrive.

Many students think and learn differently from their chronological age-mates. Students tend to understand, accept, and use their learning differences as assets when they are grouped together. When provided with consistent appropriate academic challenge, these students tend to be more comfortable with themselves (and with others).

As an example, consider the range of students who qualify for special education services. These students require teachers who have specialized training in understanding and responding to their learning needs. We would not expect all students with IEPs to receive the same interventions. Likewise, we cannot expect all students identified as gifted or as ELL students to have the same learning needs. All students have strengths and experiences that influence where they are in any curriculum and their ability to move through content that is new to them.

While students may share some traits and learning needs, in some classes, there are fewer "typical" than "atypical" learners. Gifted students who are highly and profoundly gifted, twice-exceptional, culturally and linguistically diverse, highly creative, or underachieving all learn in vastly different ways. Teachers with personal experience and/or formal training in one of these areas learn how to build on the students' strengths while addressing areas of need.

The bell curve in **figure 1.1** depicts the range of abilities found in any given classroom where purposeful student grouping, including cluster grouping, is not considered. It is exceedingly difficult for most teachers to adequately engage and challenge students within this wide spectrum. Flexibly grouping students according to specific learning objectives helps make this feat manageable for teachers.

Many students in the –2 to –3 stanines of the bell curve receive special education services. These students have special learning needs that require trained teachers with expertise in the specific needs and challenges these students may have. The same is seen in how schools group and serve their ELL students. Schools structure their schedules with these students in mind. Gifted students need the same attention. Some

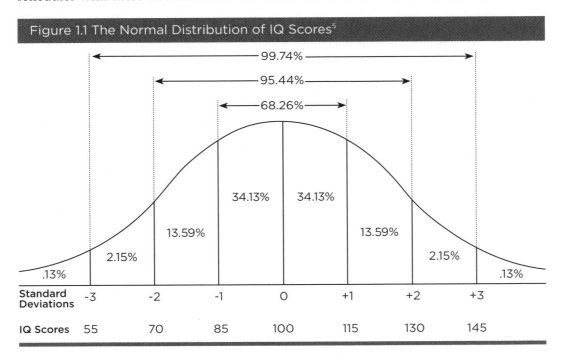

Figure 1.1 The Normal Distribution of IQ Scores[5]

5. Sattler, J. M. (1992). *Assessment of Children: WISC-III and WPPSI-R Supplement.* La Mesa, CA: Jerome M. Sattler, Publisher, Inc.

of the students in the two aforementioned groups also qualify as gifted students, though many go unidentified. Special education students who are also gifted are often referred to as twice-, multi-exceptional, or 2E learners. When we can identify giftedness in these subpopulations, we can more appropriately address all gifted students' instruction.

Regrettably, most states and the federal government fail to provide additional funding for students who qualify as gifted. This lack of funding and legislation makes it incumbent upon the schools to allocate their existing funds to ensure they are meeting the learning needs of all their students, including those with higher than average ability. Purposeful grouping with all our students can help achieve this goal, as we will discuss in the following section on cluster grouping.

The Schoolwide Cluster Grouping Model: One Example of Ability Grouping

The Schoolwide Cluster Grouping Model (SCGM) is an inclusion model in which gifted students are integrated in fixed groups into mixed-ability classes with teachers trained to provide appropriate differentiation opportunities for all students using various flexible grouping strategies. In this way, SCGM is both a fixed *and* a flexible grouping model. This specific model for providing gifted education services—when implemented with fidelity—has the potential to raise achievement for all students without requiring additional funding for the schools. In this model, *all* students in the school are strategically placed into classrooms based on their abilities, potential, or achievement with the goal of narrowing the learning range in each classroom. We chose to place special focus on the SCGM here as an example of ability grouping, since no other formal model is supported by solid research. Also, many schools implement aspects of the SCGM, if not the whole model. (**Note:** We focus on a second ability-grouping model—content replacement—in the section following this one.)

The SCGM creates a balance of ability and achievement across each grade level and yields desirable outcomes for all students. Cluster grouping can enfranchise many gifted students who previously have been left out of gifted programs, including gifted children in the primary grades, twice-exceptional students, gifted culturally and/or linguistically diverse (CLD) students, gifted students who are nonproductive or uncooperative, and students with high ability who may lack background knowledge and experiences due to poverty.[6]

Cluster grouping provides positive outcomes for schools, as it:
- Embraces diversity
- Increases achievement
- Expands gifted services
- Raises expectations for all
- Attracts and retains smart students
- Costs nothing to implement

---

6. Winebrenner, S., and Brulles, D. (2008). *The Cluster Grouping Handbook: A Schoolwide Model: How to Challenge Gifted Students and Improve Achievement for All.* Minneapolis, MN: Free Spirit Publishing.

Advantages of cluster grouping include:

- A narrowed range of abilities in the classrooms, which allows for more focused instruction

- Strategies used for advanced ability learners can be used for *all* students

- Ongoing assessment of students' strengths and needs ensures continual progress

- The ease of providing specific instructional interventions to flexible learning groups

- Gifted students are more likely to receive advanced instruction and extended learning opportunities

- Not all students are working on the same material at the same time

- Higher expectations for all students

Though little experimental or causal research on the achievement impact of cluster grouping is available, that which does exist documents equal levels of growth for all students whether or not they are identified as gifted.[7] Most other research is observational or correlational, which cannot be empirically evaluated, resulting in significant methodological limitations.

COMPOSING CLUSTER CLASSROOMS STRATEGICALLY

Classroom compositions are carefully structured with two main goals: to ensure that there is a balance of achievement and ability throughout the grade level, and to reduce the learning range found in any given classroom. This system provides opportunities for teachers to more readily respond to the needs of all their students.

The student identification categories in **figure 1.2** provide guidance for the fixed grouping of all students into classrooms. Grouping categories consist of:

Group 1—Gifted: All gifted-identified students, including those who are not fluent in English, not productive in school, and twice-exceptional gifted students.

Group 2—High Average: Highly competent and productive students who achieve well in school.

Group 3—Average: Students achieving in the average range of grade-level standards.

Group 4—Low Average: Average students who are able to achieve at grade level with support.

Group 5—Far Below Average: Students who struggle in several subject areas and score significantly below proficiency levels on academic measures.

After designating the appropriate grouping category for each student, the placement team assigns students to classrooms. The process starts by clustering all gifted-identified students into designated gifted-cluster classrooms. Next, high-average students are placed into classrooms that have not been assigned the gifted cluster. Average students are then placed evenly in all classrooms, and low-average students

7. Brulles, D., and Winebrenner, S. (January 2011). "Maximizing Gifted Students' Potential in the 21st Century." American Association of School Administrators, aasa.org; Brulles, D., Saunders, R., and Cohn, S. J. (2010). "Improving Performance for Gifted Students in a Cluster Grouping Model." *Journal for the Education of the Gifted*, 34(2), 327–350; Gentry, M. (1999). "Promoting Student Achievement and Exemplary Classroom Practices Through Cluster Grouping: A Research-Based Alternative to Heterogeneous Elementary Classrooms." Storrs, CT: University of Connecticut, National Research Center on the Gifted and Talented.

Figure 1.2 Recommended SCGM Classroom Composition for a Single Grade Level[8]					
CLASSROOM	**GIFTED STUDENTS**	**HIGH-AVERAGE STUDENTS**	**AVERAGE STUDENTS**	**LOW-AVERAGE STUDENTS**	**FAR-BELOW-AVERAGE STUDENTS**
A	6	0	12	12	0
B	0	6	12	6	6
C	0	6	12	6	6

Note: Classes A, B, and C designate three sections in one grade level. The numbers of students in each table vary.

are placed in all classrooms according to the charts. Far-below-average students are grouped in the classes that do not have the gifted cluster.

GROUPING VARIATIONS IN THE CLUSTER MODEL

Establishing the number of gifted-cluster classes at a grade level and then placing students into the various classes involves weighing and balancing various criteria. The number of gifted-identified students is the primary factor determining the number of gifted-cluster classes needed in each grade. Because these numbers change yearly, the number of gifted-cluster classes in a specific grade level may also change from one year to the next.

The text and tables that follow show examples of ways to place students in these scenarios.

Few Students for One Gifted-Cluster Classroom

Variations on the suggested model are necessary when grade levels contain few gifted-identified students. When zero to three gifted students are in a grade level, include some high-average students along with the gifted students in the gifted-cluster classroom, as seen in **figure 1.3**. The purpose is to create a balance of ability and achievement levels in all classes in the grade.

Figure 1.3 Recommended Cluster Grouping for Grades with Few Gifted Students[9]					
CLASSROOMS	**GIFTED STUDENTS**	**HIGH-AVERAGE STUDENTS**	**AVERAGE STUDENTS**	**LOW-AVERAGE STUDENTS**	**FAR-BELOW-AVERAGE STUDENTS**
A	1	7	13	9	0
B	0	10	12	5	3

Too Many Gifted Students for One Gifted-Cluster Classroom

High numbers of gifted students in one class sometimes represents a challenge for the gifted-cluster teacher. Grade levels with more than ten gifted students may want to divide the gifted students into two gifted-cluster classrooms. When there are enough gifted students to form two gifted-cluster classes, there are usually two

---

8. Adapted from *The Cluster Grouping Handbook: A Schoolwide Model: How to Challenge Gifted Students and Improve Achievement for All* by Susan Winebrenner and Dina Brulles (Minneapolis, MN: Free Spirit Publishing, 2008). Used with permission.
9. Adapted from Dina Brulles and Susan Winebrenner. "The Schoolwide Cluster Grouping Model Restructuring Gifted Education Services for the 21st Century," *Gifted Child Today, 34(4),* 35–46 (October 2011). Used with permission.

or more other section(s) in the grade level into which high-achieving students are grouped. This careful placement ensures a balance of ability and achievement levels across the grade.

When dividing gifted students into two cluster classrooms, the gifted students can be placed into the cluster classes based on their learning strengths in math or reading, as seen in **figure 1.4**. In classroom A, gifted students who are strong in math are placed with a teacher who specializes in math. In classroom B, the gifted students who are strong in language arts are grouped together. Similarly, in classrooms C and D, the students who are far below average are placed according to resource assistance provided based on the students' needs.

Figure 1.4 Recommended Cluster Grouping for Grades with Many Gifted Students[10]					
CLASSROOMS	GIFTED STUDENTS	HIGH-AVERAGE STUDENTS	AVERAGE STUDENTS	LOW-AVERAGE STUDENTS	FAR-BELOW-AVERAGE STUDENTS
A	10	0	12	12	0
B	12	0	12	10	0
C	0	16	8	4	6
D	0	16	8	4	6

Combination/Multiage Classes

Combination classes, also known as multiage, or multigrade classes, provide an ideal placement for gifted students. In multiage classes, all students work at varying challenge levels within the same content areas. In this setting, the teacher provides ongoing, formative assessment for all students to create flexible learning groups. This routine practice of preassessing students' entry levels in the content areas is ideal for the gifted students in the class.

Figure 1.5 demonstrates how a small school with one and a half sections of both second grade and third grade provides services for their gifted students using the SCGM. The school created a multigrade class as the second and third grades gifted-cluster class. High-achieving students were placed in the other classrooms in each respective grade. A similar situation was employed for fourth and fifth grades in this small school. The classes maintained the same balance as previously described.

Figure 1.5 Recommended Cluster Grouping for Multiage Classes and Related-Grade-Level Classes[11]					
CLASSROOMS	GIFTED STUDENTS	HIGH-AVERAGE STUDENTS	AVERAGE STUDENTS	LOW-AVERAGE STUDENTS	FAR-BELOW-AVERAGE STUDENTS
Grades 2–3, Multiage	3 to 5	0	5 to 6	4 to 5	0
Grade 2	0	10	9	3	6
Grade 3	0	10	9	3	6

Note: This school has 1.5 sections in grades 2 and 3.

10. Brulles and Winebrenner. (October 2011). Used with permission.
11. Brulles and Winebrenner. (October 2011). Used with permission.

Large Numbers of Both Gifted and Far-Below-Average Students in a Grade

Occasionally, grade levels have very large numbers of gifted students and far-below-average students. This scenario creates the need to place some of the far-below-average students into a gifted-cluster class. Assistance from a resource teacher helps the gifted-cluster teacher who is working with the full range of abilities in her classroom. Principals and teachers find that the cluster-grouping model facilitates the scheduling of resource teachers because the students receiving resource assistance are also clustered.

Figure 1.6 shows how one school handled this scenario. The principal separated the students in the gifted and far-below-average groups according to the students' area(s) of strength or need: in this case, mathematics. She then placed the groups with a teacher (in classroom B) who enjoyed using flexible groups to differentiate in math.

Figure 1.6 Recommended Cluster Grouping for a Grade with Many Gifted and Far-Below-Average Students[12]					
CLASSROOMS	**GIFTED STUDENTS**	**HIGH-AVERAGE STUDENTS**	**AVERAGE STUDENTS**	**LOW-AVERAGE STUDENTS**	**FAR-BELOW-AVERAGE STUDENTS**
A	8	0	10	9	0
B	6	6	10	0	5
C	0	12	6	2	7

Note: When it is necessary to combine gifted and far-below-average students in the same class, group students according to areas of need, such as mathematics.

Middle Schools That Departmentalize

Middle schools can incorporate the SCGM in several ways. The subject areas that cluster group are commonly determined by the school schedule. Some middle schools find it practical to cluster group for specific subjects, such as language arts and social studies. They then form homogenous learning groups typically based on math achievement levels and have heterogeneous classes for science and electives (see **figure 1.7**).

Figure 1.7 Recommended Cluster Grouping for Middle Schools[13]					
CLASSROOMS	**GIFTED STUDENTS**	**HIGH-AVERAGE STUDENTS**	**AVERAGE STUDENTS**	**LOW-AVERAGE STUDENTS**	**FAR-BELOW-AVERAGE STUDENTS**
A	6	0	12	12	0
B	6	0	12	12	0
C	0	6	12	6	6
D	0	6	12	6	6
E	0	6	12	6	6
F	0	6	12	6	6

---

12. Adapted from Brulles and Winebrenner. (October 2011). Used with permission.
13. Adapted from Winebrenner and Brulles. (2008). Used with permission.

FAQS ABOUT THE SCHOOLWIDE CLUSTER GROUPING MODEL[14]

What does it mean to place students in cluster groups? Gifted-identified students are placed ("clustered") into a mixed-ability classroom with a teacher who is trained to differentiate curriculum and instruction for gifted students. High achieving students are placed into fixed groups in classrooms without the gifted students. All classes in the grade level contain students of mixed abilities and use flexible grouping strategies (such as regrouping for specific instruction and within-class groups) with all students once they are clustered appropriately.

Isn't cluster grouping the same as tracking? In tracking, students are placed in fixed groups into classrooms with others of comparable ability and typically remain together throughout their school years with little opportunity for flexible grouping or differentiated instruction for particular topics. Curriculum is based on the average ability of the students in the class. When clustered, all classes have a range of abilities. Teachers modify curriculum, extend grade-level standards, and flexibly group according to the students' needs and abilities.

Why not create small groups of gifted students in all classes? The desired outcomes of clustering become greatly diminished when doing so because teachers have a full range of abilities in their classes resulting in less accountability for teachers to facilitate progress of their gifted learners. Additionally, providing appropriate teacher training to all teachers becomes difficult to schedule.

Won't the creation of a cluster group rob the other classes of academic leadership? Aren't gifted students needed in all classes, so they can help others learn? With either gifted or high-achieving students in every class, all classes have academic leaders. High-achieving students have new opportunities to become academic leaders. Ironically, gifted students do not make the best academic leaders because they make intuitive leaps and therefore do not always appear to have to work as hard as others.

How does cluster grouping fit with other inclusion models? The models are totally compatible. For ease of scheduling and to ensure that students receive appropriate instruction by properly trained teachers, schools commonly cluster special education students and ELL students according to the services they require. Gifted students' unique learning needs can be readily served by the SCGM in the same way.

Will the presence of gifted students in the classroom inhibit learning for other students? No, not when the gifted cluster is kept to a manageable size. Recommended gifted-cluster size is four to ten students. By flexibly grouping for subjects and offering learning extension opportunities to all students in the class, expectations and levels of learning rise for all.

Are gifted-cluster groups "visible" in the classroom? Gifted-cluster groups are rarely distinguishable from other groups of students in the classroom. *All* students within the SCGM move in and out of flexible learning groups according to interest, ability, and pace regarding different topics.

---

14. Adapted from Winebrenner and Brulles (2008). Used with permission.

Why do gifted students enjoy learning in a cluster-grouped classroom?
Gifted students need to spend time learning with others of like ability to experience challenge and make academic progress. They better understand their learning differences when they are with learning peers and then feel more comfortable engaging in challenging learning tasks.

What are the benefits of grouping gifted students? Gifted students' learning needs are addressed all day, every day. The model allows schools to create learning and leadership opportunities for *all* students by balancing the classrooms so there are learning role models in every class. Cluster grouping empowers classroom teachers by expanding awareness and providing preparation for teaching gifted students in a mixed-ability classroom. The use of ongoing assessment of students' strengths and needs helps ensure that all students are being challenged and experiencing academic growth. Importantly, cluster grouping helps make gifted education part of the school culture!

Content Replacement: A Second Example of Ability Grouping

Along with cluster grouping, content replacement is an effective use of flexible grouping to meet the needs of diverse learners. The content replacement model reflects a general method for grouping students for specific content instruction. This method is often represented by other names and broadly addresses a variety of grouping purposes and structures. A few common ones include:

- Grouping advanced learners for honors classes or accelerated instruction
- Forming flexibly grouped achievement-based classes
- Grouping English language learners for English language development (ELD) classes
- Grouping students with Individual Education Plans (IEPs) for special education classes
- Grouping students involved in dual language classes, such as Spanish, Mandarin, Native American languages, and others

In practice, content replacement methods do just that: they replace the general instruction with specialized instruction in specific content areas for groups of students identified for that differentiated instruction. Content replacement, regardless of the specific purpose (such as those previously listed), generally pertains to certain content areas, most typically math and reading (and/or all areas of language arts). Methods for determining which students are involved in content replacement groups vary depending on the grouping purpose.

The following sections describe grouping criteria and considerations, and identify specialized instruction used for content replacement for students in the aforementioned groups: honors classes, achievement-based classes, ELD classes, special education classes, and dual language classes.

CRITERIA AND CONSIDERATIONS FOR CONTENT REPLACEMENT GROUPS

Most methods for identifying students for specific content replacement groups involve using formal diagnostic testing administered prior to placements for each specialized group as described as follows:

Honors classes. Students participating in honors courses are typically identified according to either: 1) Gifted testing qualifications based on district and/or state or provincial criteria; 2) school achievement data or; 3) a combination of both. Schools generally offer honors classes for content replacement in mathematics or reading/language arts. Students in honors classes remain in the same honors classes for these subject(s) throughout the current school year and future school years when successfully working at the challenge level of the class coursework.

Achievement-based classes. Grade-level teacher teams form flexible class-sized learning groups for specific standards or units of study. Ideally, these class configurations change monthly or quarterly depending on results of pretests administered prior to the topics addressed. This structure is commonly used for mathematics and sometimes for language arts.

ELD classes. English language acquisition test results in most states and provinces provide data needed to identify students for participation in ELD (English language development) classes. Identified students are commonly placed in ELD classes during part of the school day for focused instruction at their specific stage of language acquisition with a teacher appropriately prepared for this instruction. When students test at the desired level to indicate proficiency, they leave this group setting to learn in mainstream classrooms.

Special education classes. Students who have an Individual Education Plan (IEP) are grouped for specific instruction according to demonstrated need in core content areas. These class placements or small group configurations are intermittent throughout the school day/week in most cases. As with ELD placements, when students no longer demonstrate need for the focused instruction, they leave this group setting to learn in mainstream classrooms.

Dual language classes. Participation in dual language classes and programs is guided by parent and student choice along with school-determined criteria. Placement generally does not involve formal testing. Students at all ability levels can usually participate in dual language classes in schools that provide this opportunity.

SPECIALIZED INSTRUCTION IN CONTENT REPLACEMENT GROUPS

Strategies for determining curriculum for these content replacement groups involve using informal formative testing administered for each specialized group throughout the instructional process, such as the following:

Honors classes. Curriculum and instruction in effective honors classes consists of accelerated learning in specific core content areas, such as mathematics and reading. Instruction emphasizes critical thinking, problem-solving, and advanced levels of rigor and complexity within the content area. In this structure at the elementary level, grade-level teams teach math and/or reading at the same time each day. The students who participate in the honors classes leave their homeroom class to attend an honors class for that content.

Achievement-based classes. In achievement-based flexibly grouped classes, grade-level teachers determine placements based on readiness levels for the content being addressed during a given time period. The teachers each guide their instruction with the student achievement data used for the class placements. For example, if diagnostic testing shows that there is an advanced group, an average group, and a below-average group within the content being addressed for that time period, the students would be assigned to the group that best correlates with their instructional needs. In most cases, there will be push-in or pullout resource assistance for some students in the below-average group, which provides additional teaching support.

ELD classes. States have independently mandated curriculum, objectives, and resources designed for the varied levels of students' language acquisition based on their testing and placement criteria. Most of this instruction is provided within the language portion of the school day. Instructional practices for ELD classes vary dramatically throughout the country according to the diverse needs of students, geography, and state policy.

Special education classes. Instruction for students receiving special education services is determined by their IEP. In most cases, several students with similar needs are grouped together for additional support in a specific content area on a daily or regular basis. Teachers further tailor instruction for students in these small groups according to students' needs documented by informal formative assessments.

Dual language classes. The school-based program usually determines the curriculum and instruction for students participating in dual language classes. Some schools offer dual language programs by scheduling partial-day second-language instruction in some of the core content areas and English (mainstream language) in the other part of the day. Other schools offer the second-language learning all day in all content areas.

There are many situations in which schools use combinations of these grouping formats for content replacement. Two of these special configurations, achievement-based and special education classes, are represented in the following scenarios.

Classroom Scenarios

Content Replacement: Achievement-Based Classes

It's ten o'clock on a Monday morning at Hollingsworth Elementary School. Students in all four third-grade homeroom classes line up for math class. Roughly three-quarters of each class walks to one of the other three third-grade classrooms, and about a quarter of each class remains in their homerooms. The teachers are beginning a unit on numerical operations.

On Friday of the previous week, the teachers of each homeroom class administered a pretest to determine the students' readiness and challenge levels within the upcoming math unit. This assessment provided teachers with the achievement data needed to place their students into learning groups for instruction on the unit. Each teacher instructs a different group level: advanced, high average, average, and low average. The teachers collaborated to determine the cutoff scores for each group level. Interestingly, they noticed that their new student groups were considerably different from the previous unit on data analysis.

Content Replacement: Special Education Classes
The third-grade special education teacher at Hollingsworth Elementary also participates in this grouping structure for the math unit. She provides pullout services for those students who qualify for small group math intervention. This regrouping structure reduces all the teachers' class sizes and enables them to deliver more focused instruction to a group with a narrowed range of ability and achievement.

Both of these content replacement scenarios represent a data–driven approach to flexible grouping that empowers teachers and allows for all students to learn at their individual challenge levels.

In Closing

This first chapter set the stage for teaching in an ability grouping structure. It provided general information on methods for grouping students, suggested various classroom and grade-level grouping configurations, and discussed how the various grouping methods impact students with an emphasis on those with special needs. We described various common grouping structures, such as fixed and flexible groupings, small- and whole-group structures, and within-class grouping and regrouping for specific instruction. We also explained several benefits of systematic grouping methods and the importance of understanding gifted students' learning needs in order to create learning groups. Finally, we shared a broad example of ability grouping using the Schoolwide Cluster Grouping Model and how this model can address the learning needs of gifted students in a heterogeneous class setting. And we also shared the example of content replacement classes, which are commonly formed based on students' achievement or ability in a unit of study or based on learners' unique language needs.

Our goal is not to convince readers of any one way to group students but to speak to the importance of making classroom placements using data for specific instructional purposes. This chapter provides the context for our next chapter in which we discuss methods for managing classrooms where students are purposefully placed in strategic learning groups.

Chart of Common Grouping Practices

Ability grouping	A generic umbrella term used to describe various methods for grouping students, such as those described in this chart. *Note:* Ability grouping includes groupings based on interest, achievement level, learning style, and other factors in addition to ability level.
Flexible grouping (or flexible learning groups)	Students are grouped and regrouped in a variety of formats for specific instructional purposes.
Fixed groups	Students remain in static assigned groups for the entire school year. Examples include both homogenous and heterogeneous groupings described below.
Homogeneous grouping	Students of similar ability are grouped together for instruction; typically used in self-contained gifted classes, content replacement or honors classes, enrichment groups, and tracking models.
Heterogeneous grouping	Students of mixed ability are grouped together for instruction; used in typical classes and in gifted-cluster classes.
Cluster grouping	Gifted students are grouped together in one class at every grade level. The cluster group is a homogeneous grouping within a heterogeneous classroom.
Whole-class groups	Students are intentionally grouped, as in the homogenous grouping of a self-contained gifted class or in a tracking model. Students may also be grouped heterogeneously, as in a typical classroom, or intentionally, as in a gifted-cluster model.
Small groups	Students are grouped together in a variety of formats, such as a gifted cluster within a classroom, a pullout group for gifted instruction or for content replacement, within-class grouping, and regrouping for specific instruction or interventions. Small groups may be formed in one grade level or across grade levels.
Within-class grouping	Similar to small groups (described above) but only within the same class. An example is a gifted student group within a gifted-cluster classroom.
Regrouping for specific instruction	Method emphasizes the specific instruction for each group, which is usually dependent upon the group's needs.

continued →

Chart of Common Grouping Practices, continued

Cooperative learning groups	A small-group setting where students are grouped intentionally for instruction. Typically include flexible groups that *may* be homogenous (like ability) or heterogeneous (varied ability) depending on the instructional purpose.
Cross-grade grouping	Students in different grade levels are grouped for specific subjects, typically math and/or reading. Students are placed based on expressed academic need to learn that subject at a different level than their own grade level.
Tracking	Students are typically grouped by achievement levels. Groups remain fixed throughout the school year (and typically beyond the school year).
Combo or multiage classes	Classes containing two grade levels within one classroom. For example, a grade 1/2 class.
Pullout groups	Students pull out of the regular classroom for focused instruction. Examples include daily content replacement, where students receive instruction in accelerated content in core academic subjects, and intermittent pullout for enrichment.

CHAPTER 2
Establishing Structure in Classrooms That Group

GUIDING QUESTIONS
- What is the teacher's role when students are working in flexible learning groups?
- How do I form learning groups? What do I do once students are grouped? How do I know if grouping is working?
- Why should I routinely regroup my students?

This chapter demonstrates how any teacher can structure, manage, and support a class so that students can learn efficiently in flexible learning groups. You will learn methods for managing differentiated learning groups and how to transform your classroom into one where differentiated learning and engaged students are the norm. Here and throughout the book, we describe methods for informally grouping students according to their interests, learning styles and preferences, background knowledge, and achievement levels.

The Role Teachers Play

Effective teachers continually monitor student progress and adjust instruction accordingly. This monitoring and adjusting involves understanding the learning needs of *all* students and adapting the curriculum and instruction in response to their evolving needs. The process requires knowing where your students are academically in various subjects and topics, while respecting their learning preferences, strengths, and areas of need. Once you have an understanding of your students' needs—including characteristics, learning requirements, and affective concerns of students with special needs—you can use this understanding to make effective instructional choices and better facilitate learning.

Your role as a teacher is to guide, facilitate, model, challenge, question, set expectations, and evaluate students' progress. With practice, these strategies become a habit of teaching, one that greatly benefits all students, from the struggling learner to the advanced one. The good news is that with flexible groups, this method of teaching can involve little prior planning and still result in improved instruction and increased student engagement.

Many teachers and school administrators recognize that flexible grouping is at the heart of an effective classroom in today's educational environment. Teachers continually create and re-create groups based on the needs of the students and the lesson objectives. This approach reflects a renewed effort to embrace and support diverse learners. As we previously noted, the criteria for creating the groups emerge from student data. And methods for managing the groups are generated by you, the teacher, based on your instructional practices. In the next sections, we introduce methods for creating flexible learning groups within a classroom and suggest many methods for managing those groups.

Forming Flexible Groups

Typically, teachers create flexible learning groups based on formative assessment results. These assessments can take many forms: they can be observational or criterion-based. The key is that they provide you with a current picture of student understanding and allow you to make immediate adjustments to the learning environment. Criteria for creating flexible grouping may include: learning styles, abilities, interests, readiness levels, and more. Methods for forming these flexible groupings are shared in chapter 1. Strategies for gathering these criteria include informal preassessment activities, such as: Quick Checks, Whiteboard Checks, Turn and Talk, Quick Write/Draw, Muddy Moments, and other informal formative assessment strategies described in chapter 3. **Figure 2.1** describes several commonly used grouping frameworks.

Figure 2.1 Common Grouping Frameworks	
GROUPING FRAMEWORK	**DESCRIPTION**
Ability-Based (More rigid)	Group students based on scores on standardized assessments of intelligence. Students with like abilities are grouped together to allow like-minded peers the opportunity to work together.
Interest-Based (Fluid)	Group students based on their interests. Tasks are created and aligned to foster and build upon student interest.
Performance-Based (Fluid)	Group students based on performance on given tasks or assessments. Placement is based on preassessment data.
Readiness-Based (Fluid)	Group students based on their readiness to engage in specific skills or activities.
Preference-Based (Fluid)	Group students based on their preferred learning modality. This encourages learners to extend their thinking and build off the ideas of others. Offer varied modes through which understanding can be demonstrated.
Objective-Based (Fluid)	Group students based on specific units of study or assignments. Grouping students based on learning objectives, as in a tier lesson format, ensures that learners are challenged appropriately.

Managing Flexible Groups

Managing flexible groups does not need to be challenging. The key is developing a method that works for you and your students. Teach your students the expectations for small-group work by establishing norms for group performance prior to grouping. Creating these norms is critical for developing routines within the learning environment. Students quickly learn your expectations and how to successfully work within their learning teams. To achieve student buy-in, involve your students in creating group norms, just as you would with other teachers in a PLC. Once norms are in place, revisit them regularly so students are reminded of the expectations for positive engagement. See the "Possible Group Expectations List" on page 50.

You can designate groups in several ways. Placing each student's name on a card, wood craft stick, or any other small item enables you to move around students easily. Set up your groups by color, letter, animal names, or other categories. Drop students' sticks into their assigned groups based on the criteria you are using for group formation. When developing procedures for creating groups, keep in mind that students need to be able to quickly identify their group placement. Here are a few commonly used methods:

- List groups on the board at the front of the room.
- Use labeled Velcro strips and name cards to display names on a felt board.
- Write names with erasable marker on laminated pocket chart cards or small whiteboards.
- Post group configurations to Google Classroom. Students can log in to learn their grouping assignments (see classroom.google.com).
- Use the Padlet app to display student groups (see padlet.com).

Classroom Scenario

Ms. Murphy uses the "Can It" strategy with her third graders. Each student has a wood craft stick with his or her name on it. Four cans are labeled with the names of their state's sports teams. When setting up flexible groups, Ms. Murphy drops the sticks into the appropriate can and then quickly calls out students' names. The team names vary frequently. For example, the Cardinals may be her highest-ability group one day and her lowest on another day.

STRUCTURING THE CLASSROOM

Prepare in advance to help provide structure and establish systems in your classroom when students work in groups. In this section, we address four primary concerns teachers share: student movement, learning noise, recordkeeping, and organizing and distributing materials.

Posting group norms in your classroom will help keep students focused. Consider having your students create their own group norms. Look at one example of group rules developed by students:

Give thoughtful feedback
Respect others and their input
On task, all of the time
Use quiet voices
Participate fully and actively
Stay with your group

Student Movement

Accept that when students are in flexible groups working on different activities in different locations, there will be movement and interaction. You need to build in routines to allow for student movement to occur in a constructive manner. The first step is to design a movement pattern within the classroom. Establishing routines in advance make the movement and noise manageable so students can work productively.

Creating a "traffic flow" can be as simple as establishing a clockwise movement pattern or setting up classroom movement protocols for students to follow. For example, "Four on the floor" means only four students up at a time, or "Not a peep while on our feet" reminds students not to disturb others when moving about the classroom.

Here are sample questions to consider related to student movement:

How students will move about the classroom
- Is there an established traffic flow?
- Are there rules for interaction?

How to choose or rotate between centers
- Are activities tiered?
- What are the time frames for the centers?

Where and when materials may be obtained
- In one central place?
- At students' tables?
- By a student assigned to a group or team?

Now, sit back and visualize your classroom for a moment. How do you see your students moving throughout the room? Are there places where movement is restricted? Do students have easy access to the various parts of the room? Think about the following questions in relation to your classroom.
- How are the desks, tables and storage areas arranged?
- What movement patterns do the students know?
- Does the structure promote ease of movement?
- Can I arrange the room to allow for more fluid movement of students?
- Where can I create a quiet place or quiet zone?

You may wonder how to avoid having too much movement in your classroom. One way, as noted previously, is to establish specific protocols to limit the number of students moving around the classroom at a given time. For some students, even necessary movement is distracting. Make accommodations to address and plan for this potentiality. Utilizing a seating option that allows some students to face away from the movement is one means of accommodating these learners. Another option is to identify a quiet work zone where students may go when trying to stay focused on a task.

TIPS FOR MANAGING STUDENT MOVEMENT BETWEEN GROUPS

- Designate students within the classroom, and within groups, to obtain and hand out materials.

- Limit the number of students who can be out of their seats at the same time.

- Provide each table group with a set of supplies.

- Post directions and objectives for each group (either on a board or at each group's table).

- Have weekly class chats to review, discuss, or modify established class rules.

- Share your procedures with parents so they can help support your classroom management structure.

Managing Learning Noise

In an effective classroom, students are actively engaged. Engagement breeds conversation, and conversation involves some level of noise. As with movement, noise can be a distracting factor for some learners, particularly those who have sensitivities. Many of these students experience acute affective concerns such as hypersensitivity, distractibility, emotional intensities, and other issues that can impede learning. The use of a quiet work zone, as discussed in the previous section, can provide an accommodation that addresses both movement and noise issues. Students should also be allowed to use headphones to block out noise while they are working.

TIPS FOR ESTABLISHING ACCEPTABLE NOISE LEVELS

Classroom and/or individual table stoplights are used as a visual cue for students. When the green light is changed to yellow, students are alerted to the fact that the noise level is getting too high and adjustments need to be made. If the appropriate adjustment is made, the yellow light is changed to green. If not, the light goes to red and students lose their opportunity to engage with each other for a predetermined amount of time.

Establish the levels of noise needed for the varied activities within the classroom. For example, level 1 designates individual work time. A partner activity requires level 2 (side-by-side conversation), while a small group activity is level 3. Prior to each learning activity, the acceptable noise level is discussed. When noise rises above the predetermined level, a one-minute "quiet out" is enacted to refocus students to an appropriate level for the activity.

Whisper bells are used to help students maintain an acceptable noise level. When student noise rises above the desired level, the whisper bells are gently rung. The soft sound of the bells is a redirect to students.

Signals to specific students are developed to support students learning how to self-monitor their voice levels. The signal must be easy to use and provide immediate and sustainable results.

Successfully establishing procedures for how students can engage with one another without disrupting learning for others takes continual training. Your students can practice noise control procedures to make the learning environment well suited to all learners. When students are unable to adjust their noise level, follow a preestablished process to temporarily suspend collaboration, such as described in the following scenario.

Classroom Scenario

As the energy level in Ms. Flores's classroom rises, so does the noise level. Ms. Flores rings the whisper bells to remind her students that the noise level has risen to an unacceptable level. Most students immediately moderate their voices, but one group fails to lower their voices to an acceptable level. As per the classroom procedure, the bells are rung again and all students in the class stop their work, turn, and look at Ms. Flores. The expectation related to noise level is revisited quickly and students return to their tasks. If the bells must be rung a third time during the activity, a predetermined consequence is put into place. In Ms. Flores's classroom, this consequence is the loss of the ability to work with partners for the remainder of the period or day.

Organizing and Distributing Materials

Organization is a key factor of managing a grouped classroom. Distribution and collection of the varied materials needed for each group is part of necessary classroom management. These procedures become highly individualized by teachers, and they typically evolve from the type of learning activity involved. Understanding that students will be working on different tasks at different times brings this need to the forefront of designing and implementing a successful learning environment.

Empower students to maintain the organization of their classrooms and their personal assignments. Do this by creating an in-class organizational system using folders or binders for student extension assignments. Students will need easy access to their extension folders, materials, other students, and work space. Develop your organizational system with students' input.

TIPS FOR ORGANIZING MATERIALS

- Involve your students in your organization procedures.
- Designate specific and clearly identified locations where students pick up and hand in materials.
- Be consistent. It is easy to be your own worst enemy when routines change frequently!
- Be creative. Explore multiple options and don't be afraid to think outside the box.

ESTABLISHING ROUTINES

Classroom management encompasses flexible teaching routines and classroom control. The terms *flexible teaching routines* and *classroom control* may seem like a dichotomy to some. Interestingly, classroom management becomes easier when teachers effectively use flexible teaching practices because students are more likely to be motivated and engaged in learning. The most common concerns that hamper developing and establishing routines in a differentiated classroom include: planning time, coming up with the activities, grading, and student accountability, which will be addressed in later chapters. Establishing routines helps teachers plan for some of these assumed obstacles.

Classroom Scenario

Ms. Andrews's sixth-grade classroom contains five more students than Ms. Torrillo's class. She runs two more reading groups and differentiates instruction in multiple subject areas. Ms. Torrillo is continually amazed at how much her partner can accomplish each day. The students are similar, the curriculum is the same, and yet Ms. Andrews's room runs like a well-oiled machine. The difference between these two classrooms is not about the ability of the two teachers; they are both skilled educators. The difference rests in the initial few weeks of the school year. During this period, Ms. Andrews builds routines, while Ms. Torrillo reviews content.

As seen with Ms. Andrews's class, the need for establishing routines within a classroom cannot be underestimated. Often teachers say, "I have so much to cover. I don't have time to spend practicing routines." The answer to this is simple: you don't have time *not* to establish routines. The time saved over the course of a school year with established routines far outweighs the time spent building and practicing them. Routines are a mainstay in a well-structured learning environment; they help balance the workload so that everyone is using time effectively. Establishing routines is essential in all classrooms regardless of students' age levels. In fact, the older and more independent the learners, the more valuable established routines can be.

We recommend building routines for following procedures at the start of the school year. Here are some examples.

- Assignment requirements
- How and where assignments will be handed in or submitted for grading
- Procedures for late work
- Location of materials for student use
- Procedures for accessing resources and supplies
- Flow pattern for student movement
- Procedures for leaving the room
- Procedures for getting support

Use the questions on "Is Your Classroom Ready to Group?" (see page 52) to help you make sure you've considered all the basic classroom routines.

Once routines are defined, it is time to start practicing. Walk students through the routine that you have chosen. Remember that routines take consistent practice. Make a game of it. Teach one or two routines the first day, adding a new routine each day. Role-playing the desired behavior helps students verbalize and visualize the process to successfully establish the routine.

Classroom Scenario

Mrs. Labella teaches a kindergarten class in which she has eight accelerated students. She uses rotating centers in her classroom. Each center has a different activity related to the same topic. Students' groups are changed after each rotation through the centers based on the purpose of the unit, the activities, and students' needs. She swaps out different levels of the same activity at her centers for her high-ability students. The classroom runs like clockwork even when Mrs. Labella is out and has a substitute teacher filling in for her.

Here are Mrs. Labella's plans to manage learning groups and centers:

9:00–11:00 Reading Block

- Send green and blue groups to their centers.
- Send purple group to their seats to start their handwriting page. Explain seatwork to red group. Send them to their seats to complete seatwork. Have purple group come back so you can explain their seatwork.
- Start your first rotation.
- When you are ready for your second rotation, send purple group back to their seats to complete their seatwork. *(Call all students to the carpet for a debrief break after the first and second rotations.)*
- Call red group to the reading table.
- Remind green and blue groups that they should start their second center.

Each rotation that follows moves the groups to another activity flow within the pattern.

GROUPS	GREEN	BLUE	PURPLE	RED
Rotation 1	Center (1)	Center (1)	Handwriting/ Reading Group	Seatwork
Rotation 2	Center (2)	Center (2)	Seatwork	Handwriting/ Reading Group
Rotation 3	Handwriting/ Reading Group	Seatwork	Center (1)	Center (1)
Rotation 4	Seatwork	Handwriting/ Reading Group	Center (2)	Center (2)

Mrs. Labella notes: "I have been fortunate to have two parent helpers assist me at the beginning of the year. While I am teaching a reading group, I have one parent assisting with the two groups doing table work and the other parent assisting with centers. This is especially helpful in the beginning of the year. Starting in November, I have one parent helper and sometimes I fly solo. When I am flying solo, my students know they need to ask a friend for help. (The only interruptions allowed when I am working with reading groups are the three Bs: blood, bellyache, bathroom.) If they are still stuck, they can ask me for help between rotations."[1]

---

1. Deanna Labella teaches at Desert Springs Elementary School in Paradise Valley Unified School District, Arizona. Quoted with permission.

LESSON PLANNING

When developing lesson plans to guide your instruction, the question we get is always the same: "Where do I begin?" Strong lesson planning starts with the standards. The standards provide the target you are trying to hit. But developing lessons that hit the target is not enough; you must also consider the learner's level of knowledge. Respecting learners' knowledge and time means not requiring them to sit through instruction of content they already have mastered.

After you have identified the standards to be addressed, pretesting is the next step in this process. The asynchronous development of the gifted learner makes pretesting vital; however, pretesting is effective for *all* students since all students can have uneven development. You cannot assume that a student knows a basic concept simply because she or he understands a more complex one. Some students make intuitive leaps in their learning. You must rely on student achievement data to address where learning gaps appear. Considering the hierarchy of knowledge shared by Dr. Richard Cash helps us make the lesson planning process a productive one. Cash states that "the brain learns most efficiently through the following three dimensions of knowledge: factual (knowing the facts), procedural (doing the tasks), and conceptual (understanding the concepts) knowledge."[2] Knowing where the learner is within this process aids you in providing next step instruction.

Classroom Scenario

Mrs. Rodes is working with her second graders on subtraction with regrouping. From her students' pretest data, she has learned that she has learners who know their subtraction facts but do not know how to address the subtraction regrouping process. Several of her students can perform the algorithm to regroup but don't understand how or why it works, so they are unable to apply it. She also has learners who can not only complete the algorithm successfully, but they are also able to explain their understandings. Her groups are formed and she is now ready to design a lesson that will meet the needs of each group of learners.

We often talk about lesson planning as a general concept, but in a differentiated classroom where students are grouped and working at varied levels, it is helpful to distinguish the different types of lesson planning. Doing so enables you to keep all students focused on a similar topic with shared goals, but at different levels depending on student needs. The following sections describe the types of lesson planning:

- Short-term planning adjusts for students' readiness and interests.
- Long-term planning provides the instructional framework.
- Unit planning integrates content across the curriculum.

Short-Term Lesson Planning

Short-term lesson planning addresses the lessons that will occur *tomorrow* based on the learning events from *today*. In many ways, short-term planning is the lifeblood of the

2. Cash, R. M. (2017). *Advancing Differentiation: Thinking and Learning for the 21st Century.* Minneapolis, MN: Free Spirit Publishing; Anderson, L. W., and Krathwohl, D. R. (2001). *A Taxonomy for Learning, Teaching, and Assessing: A Revision of Bloom's Taxonomy of Educational Objectives.* New York: Longman.

teacher who differentiates instruction. Tomorrow's small-group activities are based upon the interactions of the students today, making it critical for you to continually monitor and document student progress. We provide strategies to facilitate this process in chapter 3.

Classroom Scenario

The students in Mrs. Larkin's advanced reading group became intrigued by the role that geologists play in the prediction of earthquakes. Students engaged in spirited discussion while several began researching on their handheld devices. Based on their inquiries and discussion, Mrs. Larkin put aside the activity she had planned and instead followed the students' lead. She asked them to generate three essential questions that were driving their discussion. She then provided the group with additional nonfiction reading material so they could explore the science of how earthquakes are predicted. She assigned students to find, answer, and develop a specific number of questions. She noticed that students tended to answer the same level of questions they had created. For example, the questions developed by Andrew's group were inferential in nature: "How has humankind's ability to predict earthquakes impacted the development of land within an earthquake zone?" Another group asked, "How can buildings be constructed to withstand the damage that earthquakes cause?" When it came time to select questions to research, the group was drawn to these types of questions rather than more literal or evaluative questions. Hence, Mrs. Larkin directed these students to come back prepared to answer their inferential questions by presenting evidence-based research with sources cited.

Short-term planning requires flexibility on the teacher's part. Teachable moments, which happen when we least expect them, provide learning opportunities that should not be ignored. Some children can learn at a surprising rate or have extensive background knowledge in various areas. This prior knowledge often accelerates students through your planned instruction requiring you to adjust those plans on the fly. Ongoing formative assessments in the form of quick checks, journal responses, and exit tickets are needed for effective short-term lesson planning to ensure students are maximizing their learning time. (Formative assessment strategies are discussed in chapter 3.)

Long-Term Planning

While the planning for tomorrow often happens based on the learning that occurs today, long-range planning provides the structure that ensures students gain the competencies they need. Having a clearly developed and articulated long-range plan provides the instructional framework that allows for the flexibility necessary for short-term planning.

Establishing a long-range plan for instruction helps you and your students see the path learning will take. Without long-range lesson planning, it is easy for instruction to get off-target and result in missed content. Long-range planning also demonstrates to school administrators that teachers are following specific objective-based guidelines while also providing opportunity for flexible instruction and enriched and accelerated curriculum.

Unit Planning in a Team of Teachers

Working together, teachers can establish plans, such as unit-length plans, that will guide instruction but still allow for the flexibility needed to meet the ever-changing learning needs of students in the classroom. Each teacher can plan part of a unit and then combine all parts into a full unit. Or, teachers can each plan one full unit and then share their unit with the rest of the team. In this way, teachers can have a full semester of differentiated lesson plans for every unit. Unit planning is long-range planning that integrates content across curricular areas and addresses multiple standards. Be sure to preassess for regrouping prior to each new unit.

INSTRUCTIONAL PACING

Pacing is another way you can differentiate in learning groups. A common complaint heard from students (and sometimes their parents) is that the instructional pace is either too slow with too much review and repetition or is too fast without sufficient remediation or support. These complaints are understandable. Some students require significantly less exposure to learn new content. In fact, some students spend an entire year looking forward to when content might be new to them, only to find that the pace is still too slow and the content isn't new the following year.

- "I sat there not learning anything at all and felt that they didn't even care."
- "I felt that they expected me to sit still and not do anything but listen to others."
- "They graded me on my behavior not my content knowledge."
- "They didn't know or care about what I knew."
- "They didn't care that I wasn't learning. But I did learn to hate school early on."

Many of these comments could also be made by English language learning (ELL) students, students with special education needs, or less motivated learners. When instructional pace does not match students' learning needs, frustration can result and students can feel that learning is out of their reach. Flexible grouping helps you create an environment where the pace of instruction can be aligned with the needs of all students.

ELL students face a double challenge each day: they need to acquire the requisite skills to move forward while also learning a new language. Adjusting the pace of instruction to allow these learners time to integrate vocabulary and procedures into their working knowledge helps them move forward at a faster pace in the acquisition of both skills and language. Struggling learners and special education students may need more repetitions to achieve mastery of content. Slowing the pace and building in opportunities for more student engagement with concepts helps ensure that these learners gain the depth of understanding needed. Utilizing Dr. Norman Webb's depth of knowledge model, which categorizes the thinking levels students are required to demonstrate, teachers can instruct at Level 3: Strategic Thinking and scaffold down or up to address the needs of their learners. (See chapter 5 for more detail.)

Interestingly, some students also expressed compassion for the teachers, saying that perhaps the teachers just couldn't understand them and didn't know how to help them learn. How many of our students are thinking these same thoughts today? Consider simple ways teachers could be made aware of students' learning needs. You could send out brief articles, website links, video clips, or FAQs, or you could present for a few minutes at a staff meeting to share common myths about giftedness, students with special needs, or ELL students. The possibilities are numerous!

Classroom Scenario

Micah entered the United States with his parents three months ago from Peru. He understands more English than he speaks. His teacher, Mr. Williams, recognizes Micah's challenges in his science classroom. The content is coming at him too quickly and he is shutting down. As a proponent of flexible grouping, Mr. Williams places Micah in what he refers to as his "vocabulary first" group. Micah's group is given the vocabulary terms for the lesson ahead of time. Working with his peers and Mr. Williams, Micah defines each word, writes a sentence using the word, and draws a quick illustration of the word. Learning the vocabulary before starting any instruction on the topic helps these learners engage in the learning process more fully when Mr. Williams instructs the rest of the class in the science terminology.

Current and emerging initiatives in education support the type of instruction that we know benefits all students: rigor, critical thinking, problem-solving, project-based learning, and performance-based assessments, to name a few. These elements should all impact the instructional pace for students

ADDRESSING SOCIAL AND EMOTIONAL ISSUES

When you become familiar with affective concerns that interfere with student learning, you can prepare for these in advance. Social and emotional needs of students can significantly influence your student groupings, classroom layout, and behavior management when students work in groups. Students in any subgroup (i.e., struggling learners or those from diverse cultural backgrounds) may struggle from a social-emotional perspective. In this section, we address two primary concerns when grouping students for instructional purposes: how to manage student "meltdowns" and ways to encourage students to step up to challenges and engage in appropriately rigorous learning opportunities.

Managing Meltdowns

You can expect an occasional meltdown in any classroom, especially in those where students are grouped. The difference in a grouped classroom is that students will experience challenges they have not faced before. At other times, the meltdowns are related to internal obstacles associated with personal issues or dealing with a special education disability, which you may not understand due to lack of exposure to these students' social and emotional needs.

Common circumstances in which students may feel anxious and melt down include when they:

- Are confused
- Are emotionally charged
- Are embarrassed by not understanding what is occurring instructionally
- Experience significant asynchronous development
- Are perfectionistic and unable to maintain composure when confronted with a challenge
- Do not understand why other students do not learn like they do
- Are frustrated with the instructional pace and/or content

- Have heightened sensitivities
- Are highly intense
- Have been used to getting easy A's with little effort

In the next section, we will share strategies to support students in preventing meltdowns before they occur.

PROVIDING CHALLENGE

All students deserve the opportunity to learn new content throughout their school day. Learning should occur every day, week, month, and year that students are in school. Unfortunately, some children routinely go weeks and even months without learning anything new in their classes. The frustration created by the lack of engagement and challenge not only often results in meltdowns, but can also create poor learning habits that will need to be addressed when challenging material finally is presented. Students can only acquire study habits when they are provided with challenges that create a need to study.

Many students come to the classroom without having learned how to persevere through difficult problems. Some may feel overwhelmed by past struggles; they feel insecure with their abilities and resist making attempts to learn new material. Others are not used to struggling to learn new content, either because everything has always come easy to them or because the instruction is beyond their grasp. Some of these students may be accustomed to receiving easy A's. When faced with a learning challenge, some students will pull back rather than risk being wrong.

Students need to learn how to struggle as part of the learning process. Dr. Phil Perrone, researcher and professor at the University of Wisconsin, tells parents and teachers that we need to give our students the opportunity *not* to succeed. By this he means that we need to structure learning experiences so students will not succeed easily or consistently with little or no effort.

Classroom Scenario

Jon was a good student in high school. He earned A's and an occasional B but never found the need to open his textbooks. His teachers were frustrated by his seeming lack of effort, yet they could not refute the fact that he did know the content. Jon had no real study habits; he didn't seem to need them. Jon's first year of college went well, but as his courses increased in difficulty, Jon began to struggle. He dropped out after his third semester of college. Was he capable of succeeding in a university setting? Absolutely, but he lacked skills; he didn't know how to study, how to struggle, or how to self-regulate. But Jon's story didn't end there. He decided to take a study skills class at a local community college and returned to the university the following year. He is currently continuing his graduate studies in animal behavior.

MODELING LEARNING

Teachers commonly hear comments such as, "He's not smart; he produces nothing." "She can't seem to complete her work. She cries every time she is given a challenge." "He's just lazy, he doesn't want to do the work." Some students simply do not know how to proceed when they encounter a challenge. For many of these students, the answers have always snapped into focus. Suddenly, when faced with an unknown for the first time, they encounter uncertainty in the learning process.

Keep in mind that twice-exceptional (2E) learners and culturally and linguistically diverse learners may be needing a different modality through which to develop and share their understandings. We recommend planning for these needs in advance by identifying one differentiation strategy at a time to practice with and implement. Remember that these students need to learn "how to learn." Teaching children "how to learn," particularly when the task at hand is not simple or straightforward, takes patience on the teacher's part and a willingness to meet the learner where they are conceptually as well as emotionally.

Classroom Scenario

Piper, a very talented third grader, sits and stares at the empty page. Tears well up in her eyes as she listens to the teacher encourage students to try writing a brief story. Give it a try, sounds easy enough, but what if she isn't correct? A tear drops onto the pristine page. Piper is locked; it isn't that she doesn't want to begin working, it's that she can't. Seeing Piper's distress, her teacher kneels beside her and asks, "Piper, the page is too big and too empty, isn't it?" Piper wipes the tears and nods. "Let's try folding it into four sections, that way you can try four different approaches and choose the one you like the best." The teacher made a simple adjustment to unlock a learner.

Learning is often a process of trial and error. We do not always know in advance what will need to be modified for students until after they've started the learning process. Teaching a student how to learn is just as important as the content that will ultimately be shared with them. By modeling problem-solving steps as they arise, we model how to approach learning in general. Talking through the process with students increases their ability to independently apply the process when needed.

Most of us can think of at least one student who, when faced with a serious challenge, was unable to manage in a positive way. Students' reactions vary. Some become paralyzed into inactivity like Piper. Others disengage, have meltdowns, speak critically, act out, or even cry. The teacher needs to model what real learning looks like for these students.

It is important that students understand it's okay when they don't have the answer; that provides them the opportunity to learn something new. As SENG founder, author, and psychologist Dr. James Webb writes, we should "celebrate successive successes" with these students. We should acknowledge and respect the learning that's occurring and the progress the student is making, rather than just judging the outcome. This practice helps students understand that the process of learning is what truly matters. Teachers can model this by letting the students help develop their own learning plans. Students soon learn to let their ideas emerge in the process of addressing a difficult challenge.

MEETING *ALL* STUDENTS AT THEIR CHALLENGE LEVELS

Fear of failure can be debilitating for any learner and may prevent a perfectionistic learner from engaging in the learning process. When a learner, who has always known the answers and has been repeatedly told how bright she is, suddenly finds herself in a learning environment that challenges her, it can be terrifying not to know how to proceed. Students in this situation sometimes complain of feelings of nervousness and helplessness, withdraw from the schoolwork, or even experience anxiety attacks. Avoidance behaviors can be found in any learner approaching new material. The idea that "learning is easy" is truly a myth. Learning takes persistence, perseverance, and the willingness to take a risk; this is true for all students. Learning is hard work!

Gifted learners aren't the only ones who experience this phenomenon. Struggling learners, ELL students, and special education students also often feel left behind in a traditionally structured classroom. Content may be coming too fast or in a format that the students cannot fully access. As discussed in detail in chapter 6, differentiated instruction and scaffolded activities within the classroom allow these learners to receive the appropriate level of challenge to extend their learning experiences.

Providing consistent opportunities for all students to learn at their challenge level is both a goal and a responsibility of teachers. It's what you set out to provide to all your students. However, your students with the highest potential are the ones who usually are not challenged by the standard instruction. Curriculum, standards, and textbooks are designed for the average student. Well-funded systems are usually in place for students who are below average, but typically little to no support is available for those who are above average. Although some of these students get good grades and make the required academic progress, we need to provide interventions that will instruct these students at their personal challenge levels.

You can provide challenge in an engaging way by identifying and building on students' strengths and interests. Gifted students have deep and varied interests, and many would love the opportunity to pursue those interests through their academics. Allowing students to direct their own learning can frequently provide a more challenging and interesting project or study plan than what you had planned for them.

One goal in a differentiated classroom where students are grouped is to create an environment providing acceleration, enrichment, and rigor based on students' learning needs. In this ideal situation, students may be actively engaged in multiple activities and may not be participating in the same learning activities as the rest of the class. A teacher understands that one student's learning challenges are not the same as the challenges of others. Working with students to establish rigorous, but realistic, learning goals is a critical part of the process of creating an environment where productive struggle is expected for all students, regardless of their ability.

PARTNERING WITH PARENTS

The first time parents see their child struggling with a learning opportunity can be a frightening experience; their tendency is to step in and "save the day." Alerting parents to the value of supportive, productive struggle and the need for students to learn how to learn is very important.

Be proactive with parents and legal guardians when it comes to ability grouping students. Under-informed parents can understandably be nervous. Students from diverse cultures may have unique challenges that need to be addressed within the learning environment; however, their parents may be unfamiliar with public school systems. They may lack the ability to advocate for their child or discuss educational concerns with teachers. And some cultural norms may alter the way a learner functions within the learning environment. For example, Navajo children are taught that it is disrespectful to look an elder in the eyes. Yet in our classrooms, we say "Look at me." Understanding the culture from which a learner comes is a valuable tool to unlock the learning process and connect with families when needed.

Students with special needs face the issue of productive struggle daily. Ensuring that they are engaged in productive not destructive struggle is essential. Additionally, their parents need support in understanding ways to engage but not frustrate their child. For example, learning in small chunks is a great way to move forward learners who are struggling or who have special needs. Breaking down an assignment into manageable pieces helps eliminate being overwhelmed with the enormity of a task. This method provides the opportunity to learn each of the skills needed in semi-isolation, thus allowing for a more complete focus on the skill at hand.

You may also need to help parents of gifted students understand that intelligence does not equal effortlessness. Providing a challenging environment with high expectations is a vital part of the learning process that may have been missing for many gifted students. Students and their parents need to learn that hard work can be challenging and engaging and need not be feared.

Elementary and middle school are the best places for students to learn how to push themselves beyond the known into the unfamiliar. As a teacher, you need to share with parents, verbally and in writing, the differentiation strategies you are using so parents can help with the productive struggle process. A few avenues include a Back-to-School Night, newsletters, web pages, daily communications, and parent-teacher conferences. This constant contact will inform parents so they can better understand and support your efforts to provide appropriately challenging curriculum and instruction to their children.

Classroom Scenario

Antonio has a learning disability in reading and written communications. He sees the special education teacher daily for instructional support. Homework is always a battle. His parents want him to be successful and, in the past, have often ended up doing a good portion of his homework. This year, his teacher has implemented a new procedure for homework. "Five, I Can" gives Antonio some control over his homework. He selects five items that he feels he can successfully complete and does his best with those five items. Antonio's parents have been updated on the new approach and understand that Antonio is being assessed not on whether he is right or wrong, but on his attempts. His teacher gains a more accurate look into what Antonio can do independently, and now Antonio is learning how to manage productive struggle.

FORMING LEARNING TEAMS AND TEACHING COLLABORATION

The differentiated and grouped classroom uses the concept of team control. The tasks, materials, and time frames are varied, and in many cases a tiered assessment is used. Students work on different activities with different materials within the same topics or lessons. This type of management structure builds a team environment and empowers students. They come to rely on one another, and because they are working on the same lesson activity or project, they develop responsibility. They become problem-solvers and take ownership of the outcomes of their learning. It is this sense of ownership that you are seeking to develop when your students work in small learning groups.

Figure 2.2 Ten Tips for Productive Group Work[3]

1. Be clear with students about the reasons for, and benefits of, group work.

2. Ensure that all group members clearly understand the rules, procedures, and norms of group work.

3. Assign tasks that match group types.

4. Create groups in sizes that fit the function of the task (groups with three to five students usually work best).

5. Offer group members feedback about their performance and functioning.

6. Be flexible with the group membership; when the group is functioning below expectations, shift the membership to ensure productivity.

7. Ensure that all members feel a part of the group and have duties to fulfill.

8. Balance the group membership so students bring out the best in each other.

9. Allow the group leadership to be selected democratically, either by the teacher or the students.

10. Practice with students the effective and efficient movement in and out of the group.

Sometimes, you might structure your small groups for the purpose of forming learning teams within the classroom. These learning teams may function for a day, a week, or even a month depending on the teams' purpose. In moving from groups to learning teams, an internal group dynamic emerges. Students are part of something bigger and must work together in different ways. Learning the dynamics of teamwork is critical for students' learning process and for life in general. They learn to *collaborate,* not simply cooperate. Cooperation is an important skill to have, but peer collaboration goes beyond cooperation. For small-group learning teams to be successful, students must also learn to collaborate effectively, which is a skill that must be

---

3. Adapted from *Differentiation for Gifted Learners: Going Beyond the Basics.* Diane Heacox and Richard M. Cash (Minneapolis, MN: Free Spirit Publishing, 2014). Used with permission.

modeled, as well as taught, through direct instruction. Collaboration is the ability to work collectively toward a common goal, valuing the contributions of all and arriving at a product that represents elements of each contributor. Students engaged in collaboration persevere with a difficult task longer and overall remain more actively engaged. Collaboration supercharges performance; when learners are working on a collaborative team, they are more motivated and willing to take on challenge.

Learners of today have changed from those in traditional classrooms of the past, and it is critical that the environment changes to meet their learning needs. A differentiated classroom is one of flexible grouping and learning teams where student needs are the driving force.

Figure 2.3 Classroom Management Then and Now	
Traditional Classroom: Teacher Control	**Differentiated Classroom: Student Team Control**
Students are working on same tasks.	Student tasks are varied based on student needs.
Students are working with same material.	Materials differ in complexity.
Students are working with the same time frame.	Time frames differ depending on the tasks.
Students are assessed using the same assessment.	Tiered assessments support appropriate challenge for all learners.

Guiding and Facilitating Learning in Flexible Groups

Effective teachers often guide learning once collaborative learning teams have been formed by drawing out and building upon students' interests, ideas, and strengths. This process takes a positive and collaborative approach driven by the students and guided by the teacher. As a teacher, you learn to recognize and respond to students' cues and experiences and guide them to expand on the content being learned in a way that interests and challenges them. This typically takes place through grouped, project-based learning where students can integrate previous knowledge in various subject areas and apply that understanding to solve a new problem. Students get excited about learning in this way and quickly become engaged and engrossed in their projects. This is when real learning occurs.

Classroom Scenario

Mrs. Shapiro was beginning a unit on plants. She recognized that the students in her classroom had different strengths and weaknesses. One student, Rosario, had vast knowledge of the upcoming content. Rosario's family owned a local organic farm. Mrs. Shapiro learned that Rosario worked with his family planting and harvesting year-round. Naturally, Rosario was involved in his family's discussions about the crops, such as weather, utilities, costs, and regulations. Mrs. Shapiro documented that Rosario was proficient with the concepts and vocabulary in the unit that she planned on teaching over the next month. Two other learners, Marco and Robert, also had an understanding of the content. Engaging these three learners in a real-world project would capitalize on their current understandings, as well as provide exposure to and experience in the related fields of math and science. Each student brought a specific skill set to the project. Rosario had firsthand knowledge of an organic farm, Marco was skilled in statistics and data organization, and Robert brought marketing expertise to the group. Mrs. Shapiro facilitated a project where the boys would study some of the organic farming procedures for small farms, collect and categorize data (resources, production, planting and harvesting dates, expenses, and profit), and prepare a presentation demonstrating the farming process and discussing costs of producing plants for sale and consumption.

In the presentation, Rosario showcased his deep understanding of plants and furthered the understanding of both his teammates. Through the process, all three boys learned to create and manage a working timeline, collect and organize data, calculate profit, study weather trends, consider weather's impact on plants, research potential insect damage, and more, along with building presentation skills. The project served as a valuable learning experience and provided a real-life demonstration of learning for the whole class.

After guiding students toward learning extensions, you then facilitate the process. Facilitation can take several forms, such as:

- Creating guidelines and project criteria
- Scheduling time frames and checkpoints
- Setting expectations
- Seeking resources
- Developing an evaluation tool

This facilitative process involves you and your students. The students' participation in the process ensures buy-in and can lead them to invest more effort. The result is more engaged learning and increased productivity.

Some students are often passionate learners. They connect with content and the learning process but may be disenfranchised by traditional methods and pacing. Forcing these students to follow a standardized academic program can be problematic because their varied interests and background knowledge in certain areas drives their thinking. Involving students in the lesson design enables them to engage in all aspects of the learning process and helps direct their own learning and increase accountability.

Classroom Scenario

Mrs. Stine had been specific in her directions to Riley, Matthew, and Yuri, the three gifted fifth-grade students in her class: "Using Rubistar, create a rubric that can be used to assess our current project." The students worked together enthusiastically to create their plans and could not wait to share them with their classmates for feedback and input. Their commitment to the task was evident as they enjoyed responding to their classmates' questions and comments.

The teacher stood back (not an easy task) and watched as her students worked through the rubric, adjusting and refining it until they had a product ready for her. When asked why she would do it this way rather than simply give the students the rubric, her response was simple, "It's all about the process. The students' commitment to creating the rubric will carry through in their work on the project itself."

SETTING AND MEETING EXPECTATIONS FOR GROUPS

Differentiated learning requires that we establish expectations for students' work in advance, whether the work is completed independently or in a group format. When preparing to work on alternative projects, you and your students discuss what steps and due dates are required. You then create a simple plan outlining these steps. To establish expectations, some teachers have the parent and student sign a lesson extension contract. Working within a group dynamic takes practice, and students will need the opportunity to discuss the challenges they anticipate as well as ways they will address those challenges.

When given the opportunity to work on enriched and extended learning activities, most students quickly accept that this involves certain expectations. Students learn to set and meet expected timelines. When students working on an extended learning project have difficulties meeting the expectations, you can revisit the plan together to decide what types of support or adjustments might allow for better success. Use the "Log of Extension Activities" on page 53 to help your students track their work on these projects.

You should also set expectations for yourself. Start slowly, then continue learning and practicing new differentiated instruction throughout the school year. You might begin by adding two extension options for students and then build to three. Then add independent study. Or select one or two subjects to begin with as you learn and practice with various strategies. Teachers are notorious for demanding perfection from themselves. Diving headfirst into the deep end of the differentiation pool may at times leave you paddling to just keep your head above water.

Classroom Scenario

Mr. Parks, a second-year teacher, was sure that this year everything would fall into place. His first year was challenging as he worked hard to address the needs of the children in his classroom. He focused his differentiation efforts on mathematics, the area he identified as the greatest need. Based on his preassessments, he facilitated two to three flexible learning groups throughout the year. The groups changed frequently as students demonstrated the need for more or less instructional support.

This year, Mr. Parks planned to implement flexible grouping strategies and provide differentiation throughout the curriculum. In just a couple weeks, Mr.

Parks was overwhelmed and questioned whether he could achieve his instructional goals. He sought out assistance from another teacher at his school who reminded him of a phrase shared in a recent workshop provided by the district: "Differentiation requires practice. Little steps. Take it one subject or strategy at a time."

Set expectations for yourself to learn along with other teachers at your school, but remember what we tell our students: Perfection isn't the goal. Learning is the goal, and learning is a *process*. We don't demand perfection from our students, and we can't demand it of ourselves. Students benefit from a teacher who is willing to learn and willing to invest the time to improve instruction in the classroom.

Transition comfortably into a process where students are working in flexible learning groups in several subjects. Choose the subject area you are the most confident in and start there. Preassess, build your groups (not too many, two to four is a good number), and design differentiated instructional activities to address the different learning needs of the students. Re-assess and re-group as needed, and remember they are "flexible" learning groups; they change as your learners grow. When you are comfortable, add another subject area, one step at a time. Before you know it, flexible grouping will be a regular part of your students' learning environment.

Flexible grouping connects students to content in meaningful, respectful ways; it engages and challenges them. Successfully grouping your learners means that you are continually employing varied ways of thinking about time, materials, tasks, and groupings based on your observations of students' needs.

In Closing

This chapter began by describing the teacher's role in guiding and facilitating instruction in classrooms that employ grouping methods. We discussed and provided examples of how you can establish routines, provide structure, and plan lessons in classes where students learn at their various challenge levels. We examined classroom procedural considerations such as movement, noise level, expectations, and recordkeeping to support classroom management when students work in groups. We then offered suggestions on how to group and facilitate learning with a goal toward building a productive group work environment. Together, these aspects work to create a supportive learning environment where all students can be engaged and challenged.

Possible Group Expectations List

- Listen carefully.

- Respect the ideas of others.

- Make sure everyone has a turn to speak.

- Do not use put-downs or discouraging words; be positive.

- Give reasons for your opinions.

- Monitor your voice levels.

- Signal that your group has a question by all group members raising their hands.

- Stay on task by using your form: **Goal Setting: One Day/Week at a Time**.

Goal Setting: One Day/Week at a Time

Student's Name _____

Start Date _____

DATE	GOALS	WORK ACCOMPLISHED

Adapted from *The Cluster Grouping Handbook: A Schoolwide Model: How to Challenge Gifted Students and Improve Achievement for All* by Susan Winebrenner, M.S., and Dina Brulles, Ph.D., Free Spirit Publishing, 2008. Used with permission.

Is Your Classroom Ready to Group?

ASSIGNMENT PROCEDURES

- Are assignment guidelines posted?

- When and where will students hand in work?

- How will late assignments be handled?

MATERIALS

- Where will materials be located?

- Will all students have access or only one student per group?

CLASSROOM MOVEMENT

- Do you have an established traffic pattern in your room?

- Do students know your expectations for moving about the room?

- What are the procedures for students leaving the room?

LEARNING ENVIRONMENT

- Does the room arrangement facilitate group work?

- Is there a place for individual students to work?

- Is there a quiet zone?

GETTING SUPPORT

- What is the procedure for getting support when the teacher is occupied?

- How do groups notify the teacher that support is needed?

Log of Extension Activities

Student's Name _____ Start Date_____

Topic of Study _____

TODAY'S DATE	MY PLAN FOR THIS PERIOD	WHAT I COMPLETED TODAY

Adapted from *The Cluster Grouping Handbook: A Schoolwide Model: How to Challenge Gifted Students and Improve Achievement for All* by Susan Winebrenner, M.S., and Dina Brulles, Ph.D., Free Spirit Publishing, 2008. Used with permission.

CHAPTER 3
Assessment and Flexible Grouping

GUIDING QUESTIONS

- How do I know which assessments to use before, during, and after group instruction and how do I use the results of those assessments?
- How do I grade students who are working at different levels and in different groups?
- How do I communicate progress to parents when students are learning at different grade levels?

Documenting student progress in grouping models requires routinely collecting and analyzing data, which is needed to gauge success in any learning environment. Here, the data is used to monitor progress, create student placements, and regroup students when needed. In this chapter, we discuss how to accomplish this at all levels: in the classroom, at the school level, and throughout the school district.

Assessments come in many shapes and sizes. How you use the data is as important as the data itself. In the following sections, you'll find several types of assessments and grading options as they relate to various student groupings. Included are methods for analyzing student achievement and progress daily, monthly, and annually using formal and informal methods; diagnostic, formative, and summative assessments; and school and state level data. Also included are methods for grading students who are working on accelerated and/or differentiated schoolwork and for creating forms that document progress. Finally, we recommend parent reporting methods that document academic growth for students working in grouping models.

Why Assess?

The phrase "assessment drives instruction" has been used for a number of years. Yet we must ask ourselves: does assessment routinely drive the instructional practices in today's classrooms and schools? Valid assessments are critical for meeting the unique and varied needs of today's learners.

Assessment data can be used to:

- Discern strengths and learning levels of all students
- Group students for instruction
- Determine curriculum levels and instruction methods for advanced learners
- Scaffold student learning
- Assess the effectiveness of a particular teaching method

- Provide an accurate means of sharing student progress with parents
- Assist in decision-making at the classroom, school, and district level

When structured and used astutely, assessments provide information regarding student needs as well as areas of strengths. **Diagnostic assessments**, or **preassessments**, are a vital component of the teaching and learning cycle within today's multi-ability classroom. The most commonly used informal diagnostic assessments are pretests, self-assessments, and interviews. When teaching in a setting with different student groupings, we recommend having the entire class participate in the preassessment prior to beginning a new unit or project. This provides the data to form your instructional groups.

This chapter also describes informal **formative assessments** used for monitoring progress and making adjustments throughout the learning process. These strategies are particularly effective when used within small groups. Since each group will be working on different activities, the methods and times to provide formative assessments will also vary. Informal formative assessments can include commonplace methods such as conversations, journal reflections, observations, and homework. You will find that many strategies work well for multiple purposes. You can obtain different information depending on how and when the strategies are used.

Finally, **summative assessments** are tools for gauging student mastery of the content that has been taught. An easy way to think of formative and summative assessments is to relate it to cooking. Formative assessment happens in the kitchen as the cook (teacher) adds ingredients and continually tastes the food; throughout the process, the cook makes changes to enhance the taste. Summative assessment occurs when the food leaves the kitchen and is served. Once served, the cook cannot make further enhancements. Both types of assessment are needed to support the current process and to guide future instruction.

Figure 3.1 shows various types of assessments and how they might be used in a classroom to support the learning process.

Figure 3.1 Types of Assessments		
ASSESSMENT TYPE	**DESCRIPTION**	**EXAMPLES**
Diagnostic	Given at beginning of unit or year to quantify what students know about a topic	Pretests Self-assessments Interviews Surveys
Formative	Given along the way to determine how students are progressing Used by both teacher and student to impact future instruction/learning	Observations Homework Reflection journals Exit tickets Conferences
Summative	Given at the end of the unit or year to determine students' mastery of a topic after learning has occurred	Unit exams Final exams Projects Performances District, state exams

Seven Processes for Using Assessment

Before diving into the three assessment types and examples, let's look at several of the processes involved when using assessments. These processes are tools to help you guide, monitor, and document student progress. The seven processes described in this section are laid out in the natural order in which they are used in the classroom. They include:

1. Using learning progressions to guide instruction

2. Assessing academic progress along the way

3. Creating a recordkeeping system that will allow you to monitor progress

4. Recording preassessment data to document entry points

5. Grading

6. Communicating goals, expectations, and feedback

7. Constructing and deconstructing rubrics to evaluate progress in specific lessons

PROCESS 1: LEARNING PROGRESSIONS

Assessment begins with learning progressions, a component of the standards. A learning progression is a road or pathway that students travel as they progress toward mastery of the skills needed to further their education. Each road is a collection of building blocks defined by content standards for a subject. Along the road are many major mile markers; these mile markers are the foundational content standards students will need to master as they progress toward mastery of more sophisticated skills. The mile markers show what comes before and after points along the road. Although not always linear, they articulate forward movement.

Learning progressions help teachers determine whether students have navigated successfully through the mile markers and are able to move forward along the road to more advanced educational experiences. The progressions help teachers identify students who have navigated beyond the mile markers for each course and are in need of accelerated curriculum or those who need to revisit a particular location on the learning route.

Learning progressions help students see the "road map" they will be traveling prior to embarking on their journey. Without these progressions, it is easy to get lost in activities that, while fun, do not specifically align with the standard. Equally, it is our role as educators to identify the "rest stops" along the way that ensure students are on the right path.

Classroom Scenario

Kimberly, a fifth-grade student, clearly showed that this "road map" metaphor was working. When talking with her teacher about the upcoming assessment, she stated, "I like knowing where we are headed in this class, but most of all I like knowing that when we pause at a rest stop, even if we have taken a side road, you won't leave us behind."

This kind of trust is essential if students are going to feel confident in taking the necessary academic risks that are part of learning. The road map supports students in goal setting, building accountability, and taking charge of their learning environment. Learning progressions also help you feel confident that all your students are working toward an understood goal.

PROCESS 2: ASSESSING ACADEMIC PROGRESS

"If there isn't a grade attached to it, how do I get my students to do it?" This question is often asked by teachers who are implementing extension menus. Extension menus offer all learners the opportunity to connect with the content in a different way. Students can choose the extension that addresses their learning style or challenge level. Extension menu activities can be offered to students individually or in a group format. How do you get students to the point where it isn't about the grade they receive but about the learning that occurs? It doesn't happen overnight. Building intrinsic motivation comes with time and trust; these two elements are key to supporting students on their learning journeys.

The journey begins with involving your students in the process of designing how they will share their understandings of the concepts and standards to be addressed. Assign students to groups and ask questions that engage them in the process. For example, "How would you like to demonstrate your understanding of this concept?" "What will you do to express your level of knowledge of these objectives?" Then, listen to their answers and consider their ideas. You will be amazed and excited by the ideas your students share, and they will have immediate buy-in when you incorporate their ideas.

Setting the expectations for each of the extension opportunities can also be a joint process. To help students gain confidence in their ability to demonstrate their understanding, make sure that these expectations are clearly defined for all parties. Support your students by documenting their efforts in addition to monitoring their academic progress.

Preparing students for the format of the assessment helps obtain a valid indicator of their understandings. For example, if there are time constraints on a test, practice similar tasks that have a similar time constraint, so students experience the pressure of working in that format and time frame. Remember, any assessment is a snapshot of student performance, and getting a clear snapshot can be a challenge. Whenever possible, make your decisions based on multiple data points rather than on a single assessment.

Extension activities challenge students to go beyond that grade-level standard, to go deeper into the content than the grade-level standard requires, and to think about the content at a deeper level and in a more complex manner. So grading for lesson extensions should not produce a grade that is lower than their demonstration of grade-level mastery. The grade for extension activities should be based on the effort the student put into the extension. Consider the situation in Mrs. Sawyer's class.

Classroom Scenario

Caroline, a fifth-grade student in Mrs. Sawyer's class, was hesitant to attempt the extension activities provided by her teacher. It was evident to Mrs. Sawyer that Caroline was capable of moving beyond the standard assignment yet rarely did she choose to challenge herself. A conversation with Caroline revealed that in previous learning environments, she had chosen to complete extension activities but because the activities were much more complex, she was not able to earn an A. The lower scores were averaged into Caroline's grade, which resulted in her receiving a B for the class. She felt punished for attempting the more challenging assignments.

PROCESS 3:
CREATING A RECORDKEEPING SYSTEM

Creating a recordkeeping system is crucial for accumulating and recording data on the varied learning activities, standards, and assessments in a differentiated, grouped classroom. You use the data to develop lessons that can advance the learning of all students when flexibly grouping. Data from your recordkeeping system can also be used to inform parents about how you determine your different student groupings. (See more on sharing with parents at the end of this chapter on page 81.)

When developing a recordkeeping system, begin with the grade-level standards to be mastered, assessed, and documented. As mastery is demonstrated, move students quickly on to the next levels. Document where students' mastery levels are in the different content areas. Then, use that data to form their flexible learning groups and create lesson plans accordingly.

Figure 3.2 shows an example of one teacher's recordkeeping system for organizing flexible groups. This teacher uses a simple roster format. Student names are listed along with dates of formative assessments: quick quizzes, discussions, observations, and others.

Figure 3.2 Sample Recordkeeping System for Flexible Groups					
ELA, LANGUAGE	**3.1A**	**3.1B**	**3.1C**	**3.1D**	**3.2A**
Andrew A.	–	–	–	✓	–
Kyle B.	+	+	+	+	✓
Alicia B.	✓	✓	–	+	–
Brett D.	+	+	+	+	✓
Olivia F.	✓	+	✓	✓	✓
Angie F.	–	✓	–	✓	✓
Maggie H.	✓	✓	–	–	✓
Tyler J.	✓	+	+	✓	✓
Maricella M.	✓	+	✓	✓	✓
Summer M.	✓	+	✓	✓	✓
Ryan M.	+	+	+	✓	+
Jonathan R.	+	+	✓	+	✓
Miguel R.	✓	✓	✓	✓	–
Marcus S.	+	+	✓	–	–

Data is entered as follows:

- A line (−) designates a student with limited understanding of the content.
- A check mark (✓) indicates that a student is near mastery.
- A plus (+) designates a student who has mastered the content.

As assessment continues:

- Check marks (✓) added to lines (−) demonstrate an increase in understanding (✔).
- A vertical line drawn through the check mark (making a ✔) designates a student who has moved to mastery.

Though an essential part of the grouping process, recordkeeping must meet your needs as a teacher. A recordkeeping system that is overwhelming in complexity is doomed from the start. Promote ownership for student learning by involving your students in the recordkeeping process. See **figure 3.3** for ideas.

Figure 3.3 Recordkeeping Format Ideas		
FORMAT	**DESCRIPTION**	**FACILITATED BY**
By Standard (with roster)	Using a spreadsheet, student names are listed vertically down one column with standards listed horizontally across the top	Teacher
By Standard	Standards are listed in a table format; student names are added as mastery is achieved	Teacher
By Unit	Unit tasks are identified, and student progress recorded in roster format	Teacher
By Student	Standard mastery charts are created for each student. Original is kept in teacher data notebook; copy is kept and updated by student	Teacher and students
Two-Column Journal	Two-column journal format; skills and procedures are listed in "I am learning to . . . " then dated and moved to "I can . . . " column	Teacher and students; students held accountable for items in "I can . . . " column
Anecdotal Records	Observational records kept on individual and/or groups of students; summarized weekly	Teacher

Keeping Records and Charting Growth

Involve your students in the recordkeeping process to help them understand where they are on their individual continuum of learning in the various areas. This metacognitive process builds discipline and supports students' planning. Students should also be able to discuss how the activities they are working on is enhancing their understanding of the content.

Practice by having students ask themselves the following questions:

- What is the objective or purpose (of the activity)?

- What more am I trying to learn?

- What is my plan and how does this extend and deepen my understanding of the concept?

- How will I show what I have learned?

PROCESS 4: RECORDING PREASSESSMENT DATA

Preassessment only has value when the data is utilized to drive instruction. Preassessment data kept in a folder only to be pulled out to compare with post-assessments is of little value to you and of no value to your students. The data needs to be generated in a manner that makes it easily accessible and usable. The most usable preassessments are those that you can tie to specific learning targets and objectives.

The score on an assessment is not as valuable as how it was generated. Knowing that three students scored 14/20 on a preassessment is only useful if you can identify which targets or objectives the students understand and which need further development. Assessing a select number of targets allows you to focus instruction. With formative assessments, you can check off targets as they are addressed.

PROCESS 5: GRADING

Grades should reflect a student's demonstrated degree of mastery of the standard. Grades should never be punitive or seek to demoralize students; rather, they should be an accurate reflection of mastery. When formative assessments are included in grade averages, they can alter the accuracy of information shared.

Many grading systems use an average or weighted average to determine student grades. When using this type of system, be careful that students are not punished for learning material less quickly than others or for losing interest in tasks because they already know the material.

Grouping students together who already know a significant part of the content supports learning. It maintains engagement with the content as the students collaborate and share ideas while working on challenging lesson extension activities. Likewise, allowing students in need of more time or practice to work together provides them an opportunity to work without the pressure of students who are ready to move onto to new content. This flexibility supports the learning of all students.

The scenario on page 61 highlights dynamics that can occur when assessments and activities are averaged into a final grade. This scenario plays itself out in far too many learning situations. For this reason, grades must be based on grade-level standards and expectations. Attempting more complex and challenging work should never punish the learner with lower grading than what would have been earned on less challenging work. Similarly, a student who takes more time to get to the mastery level should not be penalized by using formative assessments in the grading process. Notes describing the student's performance and progress on the more complex work can be documented in narrative form. In **figure 3.4**, narrative examples show how student performance can be documented when a student is working on tasks that are outside of the regular curriculum.

Classroom Scenario

Look at these scores from Mr. Markin's fourth-grade math class:

STUDENT	PRETEST	ACTIVITY 1	ACTIVITY 2	QUIZ	ACTIVITY 3	ACTIVITY 4	ACTIVITY 5	FINAL QUIZ	GRADE
A	9/20	82%	75%	91%	68%	75%	69%	93%	79% C
B	6/20	57%	59%	63%	78%	83%	88%	96%	74% C
C	10/20	85%	93%	75%	90%	87%	95%	70%	85% B
D	4/20	80%	89%	84%	56%	67%	73%	82%	76% C

Note that both student A and student C demonstrated they knew approximately half of the content prior to instruction. As students moved through the activities, you can see several interesting dynamics. Student A appears to have lost interest in the instructional process midway through the unit. This student demonstrated clear understanding of the content on the final summative quiz, yet due to the system of averaging the formative activities into the final grade, the student received a C.

This system punishes the student who already knew material and should have been compacted out of those activities. Student B entered the learning cycle knowing about a fourth of the content to be addressed. Scores would seem to indicate that the student learned material at a slower pace than peers, yet in the final summative quiz demonstrated mastery of the content. Again, the process of averaging formative assessments into the final grade punishes this student.

As we look at the scores for student C, we see a different picture. This learner seemed to excel when the pressure was off but struggled on assessments. Mr. Markin examined his summative assessment to ensure that there was correlation between the formative assessments and the summative. Additionally, he noted that this pattern existed for student C in multiple subject areas. Test anxiety may be a factor for this learner, a topic that Mr. Markin felt worth exploring.

Finally, we look at student D. Of the four learners, this student came into the learning cycle with the least prior knowledge. The student struggled with the second set of formative activities; however, the final summative quiz indicated that the student had developed a grasp of the content. Note that the final grade does not reflect this high degree of understanding demonstrated by student D on the summative assessment.

Figure 3.4 Performance Narratives

SUBJECT AREA	EXAMPLES
Math	Tyler demonstrated mastery at 90% or higher on the 1st semester 3rd-grade math concepts. He is currently working at a 4th-grade level on these concepts. He is developing excellent problem-solving skills, both through critical and creative problem-solving structures.
Reading	Mia's grasp of nonfiction text structures places her significantly above grade level. She is currently working a full grade level above in vocabulary. She compacted out of the 5th-grade figurative language unit and is working on an extension lesson: the creation of a figurative language website.
Social Studies	Rhett continues to demonstrate a strong understanding of the 2nd-grade curriculum. His background knowledge about Native American cultures is extensive. He is working with his collaborative team on researching a culture that parallels one of the tribes studied.
Science	Katelyn demonstrated mastery of the Earth science standards for 3rd grade at 73%. Based on this assessment data, she was provided a Study Guide Contract that allows her to bypass content she already knows and participate in instruction only on material of which she has not yet mastered. She continues to show her enthusiasm and excitement for science concepts.

THE GOOD NEWS ON GRADING

Grades should reflect progress toward a goal, and the primary goal must be the mastery of grade-level standards. Therefore, the primary goal when grading should be documentation of those standards. Routinely incorporating diagnostic and formative assessments into instruction allows students to move beyond grade-level standards and delve deeper into the curriculum or related topics. The test results serve as evidence of mastery of grade-level standards; this becomes the student's grade.

If you are like many teachers, you may struggle with the amount of time spent grading. However, there is no direct correlation between student achievement and the amount of time a teacher spends grading. But there *is* a strong correlation between student achievement and the amount of time spent planning. Planning is proactive, and grading is reactive.

Spending more time planning (and less time grading) creates more engaging learning opportunities for students. Ask yourself, "How would I rather spend my time?"

Given the current pressures of accountability, it is easy to understand why you may feel overwhelmed with grading. At this point, we should make the distinction between assessment and grading. Assessment is a process; grading is the *reporting* of aspects of the process. Assessment is ongoing and guides daily grouping structures and instruction within the classroom. Keeping assessment and grading separate is an important part of the overall process and goal.

As noted previously, you can assess students informally to group them throughout the day or week so that their specific learning needs are being met. This is especially true when regrouping students for different tasks or varied task complexity. It is natural to feel the pressure to show grades for every learning activity your students complete. However, providing students feedback or the ability to self-evaluate using a rubric yields much more information about task performance. This process guides your future instruction more precisely than simply giving a student a grade.

You might feel that every time you assess, it should be a test with numerous questions, the test should be written out, and the assessment needs to be graded and recorded. However, instead of grading every activity your students complete, provide students with consistent, constructive feedback to support them in gauging their progress toward a goal. Grading each task is not necessary if students are receiving reliable feedback on their work throughout the week.

PROCESS 6: COMMUNICATING GOALS, EXPECTATIONS, AND FEEDBACK

Another critical aspect for classrooms that group is identifying and communicating goals and expectations. With a clear and accurate understanding of the learning goals and objectives, students can take ownership of their learning. For this to occur, you need to share standards and objectives daily with students in "kid speak," not educational jargon.

When you provide feedback to students about assessments, make sure the feedback is evidence-based and links specifically to learning outcomes. Feedback needs to be learner-specific to have value to the student. Comments of "Good job," "Nice work," and "Good effort" don't tell the learner what will improve future performance, nor do these types of comments inform the learner of what specifically they are doing well. **Figure 3.5** shows ways in which teachers can make feedback specific and valuable to the learner. Sharing specifics about student performance demonstrates that the teacher values the progress of the learner.

Figure 3.5 Examples of Specific Student Feedback	
INSTEAD OF THIS . . .	**TRY THIS . . . (BE SPECIFIC IN YOUR FEEDBACK)**
Good job	■ I like your word choice on this assignment. ■ Your examples do a good job of representing your ideas.
Nice work	■ You did an excellent job at showing your work on these problems. ■ The layout you chose for this assignment allows you to keep your thoughts organized and concise.
Good effort	■ Your outline was detailed and clear, but in the writing, you left out the information from Section II B. ■ I love your energy! Your verbiage gives a vivid picture of your thoughts.
Super!	■ I am excited to see that you chose to enhance your work with the detailed graphic. ■ Your explanations show a clear understanding of the problems.
Great group work	■ Your team worked collaboratively today to create the outline that will guide your presentation development. Each team member contributed to the process and your work is really a representation of everyone's ideas. ■ Your group was totally engaged in the process of creating your podcast. All group members participated and were able to share their understandings.

Feedback is also essential to support strong group dynamics. As with the individual learner, feedback to the group must be specific and clearly outline defined expectations. Whether the group is working well or struggling, feedback provides a guide for the group when extending their understandings.

Classroom Scenario

Andrew's group has been struggling to meet deadlines. The team has difficulty moving forward on tasks and often wastes valuable work time. Ms. Rios, their teacher, has met with the team on two different occasions to facilitate dialogue. She decided to set up a camera to capture the team's next session. The team was asked to review their group norms and then view the video without comment. At the end they would have a chance to share their thoughts. One student, Connor, was unable to wait and asked to have the video stopped. He turned to his fellow teammates and shared that he owed the team an apology. "I have been interrupting and talking over the top of everyone. I know you have all shared that it is a problem, I just didn't realize it until now. I will do better." The video offered the team an authentic look at their performance, allowing each team member to assess and make the needed adjustments.

Peer assessment and self-assessments provide valuable opportunities for students to take ownership of their work, whether they're working independently or in a small group. Learning to reflect on the process of acquiring new information, as well as the strategies for using information, gives students opportunities to develop metacognitive thinking. This reflection process makes it possible for students to set goals for future performance.

Assessment, at its best, is a collaboration between student and teacher. The collaboration is a partnership that seeks to create the best and most engaging learning environment for students at their own learning levels. Knowing the learning levels of all your students informs how you group them and provides information that enables you to modify the curriculum and instruction in response to your students' learning needs.

As noted previously, learning is a process; yet, oftentimes, we only assess the product or end result, rather than the journey leading to that end product. Assessment strategies also offer a means of looking at the process in addition to the product. The following sections offer a few strategies designed to encourage your students to enjoy completing quality work, while lightening the burden of grading for you.

Strategy: It's Time to Roll

This strategy is often a huge hit with students and helps support the completion of assignments. It has been proven to increase the quality of student work while decreasing the amount of time you spend grading. For this first elementary example, we will focus on using Michael Clay Thompson's book, *Caesar's English 2*. Working with a set of Latin stems or vocabulary terms, students complete a different activity every day over a six-day period. On day seven, they play a game called, "It's Time to Roll." The secondary example that follows focuses on Mrs. Chandler's ninth-grade Honors English class. *Note:* You may find the need to run out and purchase a set of multiple-sided dice!

Classroom Scenario: Elementary

For this strategy, Mr. Nguyen uses a six-sided die. Over the course of six days, his students complete six different activities with the set of Latin stems or vocabulary terms they are studying. As a group, the class numbers each of the six activities they have completed. Mr. Nguyen sets the tone by starting the activity listening to Elvis Presley's "Shake, Rattle, and Roll." A student is then selected to roll the die. The number that comes up correlates with one of the six lessons completed. This is the lesson Mr. Nguyen grades from the set of six activities. If students didn't complete some of the activities, they are hoping the die doesn't land on one of those activities!

Classroom Scenario: Secondary

Mrs. Chandler teaches ninth-grade Honors English. Each year her students work in learning groups to write a research paper, which evolves over time. She teaches components such as validating research sources, developing a thesis statement, creating an outline, and organizing a structure. Each component is broken into checkpoints that can be assessed. Mrs. Chandler uses the "It's Time to Roll" strategy to determine which components of the multileveled project she will assess at any given time.

Each component of the project is given a number from one to nine. On Wednesday of each week, students roll a nine-sided die to determine which aspect or component of the paper Mrs. Chandler will assess. Since development of the components is ongoing, Mrs. Chandler can assess the progress her student groups are making as they journey through the project. The students never know which number the die will choose, so they have to put forth their best effort on every activity. The class reviews the other eight assignments as a group, while each student self-corrects his or her own paper.

Strategy: Divide and Conquer

To introduce this strategy, use a typical math lesson. Assign your students fifteen problems and instruct them to turn in their assignments as usual. Select a student (or several students) to roll a fifteen-sided die three times. Say the die lands on five, eight, and twelve. Write these three problems on the board for the students to complete. Of the fifteen problems, these are the ones you will grade. Students who completed the homework already have solved these problems so solving them a second time should be relatively easy.

What about students who looked at the assignment, decided it was too easy, and chose not to complete it? Remember that homework is for practice. If any students truly understood the material, then they would not have needed to complete the assignment to solve the three selected problems successfully. Some students probably looked over the problems and completed the ones they were unsure of, and others probably completed all the problems. The goal is to give students the amount of practice they need and to place ownership for the learning on the learner. As with the previous example, the teacher will want to review all or some of the problems together as a class to address and correct any misunderstandings.

Strategy: Assess Yourself (and Your Friends)

Students must learn how to assess themselves and their peers. Teach your students this skill by guiding them on using rubrics to help answer these questions:

- How do I know this is complete?
- How do I know if I included all the necessary components of this lesson?
- How can I improve my work?

Using rubrics requires students to review and analyze their work, which leads to improvements. Help students learn how to use this process by demonstrating the need to go back over their work to evaluate each part. Self- and peer-assessments provide opportunities for students to develop metacognitive thinking about their learning. Assessments allow students to take responsibility for their learning as they evaluate their progress.

Nearly every project can be assessed using some type of rubric. At times you will want to create the rubric yourself and at other times you will want to guide your students to develop their own rubrics. When students provide input into how their projects are developed, they should also help develop the rubric for assessment. Require your learning teams to self-evaluate using the project grading rubric prior to submitting their projects. Have students record the team's self-evaluation on the rubric and submit it to you. Consider using a tool such as a Google Forms to create a survey format to do this.

PROCESS 7: CONSTRUCTING AND DECONSTRUCTING RUBRICS

Constructing a rubric does not have to be a daunting task. Many resource sites are available to support you in the process, such as RubiStar (rubistar.4teachers.org) and iRubric (rcampus.com/indexrubric.cfm). Learning to create rubrics is like learning anything valuable; it takes an initial time investment. Once the task becomes second nature, it actually saves time while creating a higher-quality student product. The following steps and sample rubric in **figure 3.6** will help you get started:

1. Determine the concepts to be taught. What are the essential learning objectives?

2. Choose the criteria to be evaluated. Name the evidence to be produced.

3. Develop a grid or template. Enter the concepts and criteria.

Figure 3.6 Sample Fiction-Writing Content Rubric				
CRITERIA	**4**	**3**	**2**	**1**
PLOT: "What" and "Why"	Both elements are fully developed.	One of the elements is fully developed, and the less developed element is at least addressed.	Both elments are addressed but not fully developed.	Only one element is addressed.
SETTING: "When" and "Where"	Both elements are fully developed.	One of the elements is fully developed, and the less developed element is at least addressed.	Both elments are addressed but not fully developed.	Only one element is addressed.
CHARACTERS: "Who" as described by behavior, appearance, personality, and character traits	The main characters are fully developed with much descriptive detail. All elements are discussed. The reader has a vivid image of the characters.	The main characters are developed with some descriptive detail. Fewer than three elements are discussed. The reader has a vague idea of the characters.	The main characters are identified by name only.	None of the characters are developed or named.

In the example shown, the concepts include the plot, setting, and characters. The criteria are the "who, what, where, when, and why" parts of the story. The grid or template provides a physical layout for the rubric. It is your role to determine what score will be required for mastery. For instance, if all three concepts are emphasized, a 3 in all concepts might be required for a demonstration of mastery. Students scoring a 4 in concepts demonstrate an advanced understanding of the content. If any concept of the story falls below a score of 3, then that concept would need to be retaught and rewritten with specific teacher feedback.

Deconstructing the rubric is part of the process of self-assessing. This process supports students' understanding of exactly what the teacher is looking for.

Steps to Deconstructing a Rubric

1. Start with the rubric and a packet of small sticky notes for each student. Each student will have the opportunity to make notes and mark the rubric with key information shared by you and the group.

2. With the rubric on display for students, begin with the first element to be assessed. Identify the key features needed to score "exceeds expectations" versus "meets expectations." Allow students to share their thoughts and ideas on each element with facilitative support from you.

3. Define each element one by one. When completed, students should have sticky notes on each element with key information to support them as they develop their project or assess the project of a peer. Consider providing students with a clear sleeve or folder in which to keep the rubric so that sticky notes are not lost.

Three Types of Assessment

Incorporating preassessment and formative and summative assessments plays a critical role when working with students in grouping configurations. In this section, we demonstrate why and how each assessment type serves a different purpose. We share easy-to-use examples of preassessments you can use immediately and routinely to form flexible learning groups. We then provide examples of how to use formative assessments to guide instruction within the groups and assess progress throughout the learning process. Lastly, you will learn how summative assessments provide evidence of student mastery overall and inform you of past and future grouping efforts.

Additionally, in a multi-ability classroom, you need to use out-of-level assessments to ensure that all learners are being challenged appropriately. Documentation is paramount when using these assessments to build learning groups. Initially, record student performance on grade-level standards. Once students have demonstrated mastery of the grade-level content, then begin the out-of-level assessment process. Documentation continues as you identify the above-level standards students have mastered, as well as those for which the students need further learning opportunities. For high-ability learners, it will often be in the "above-level" standards where you can document their growth. This process of compacting the students out of material already learned helps ensure that students engage in material at a level that promotes productive struggle. Documenting and being able to justify student placement in advanced material to both administration and parents is a necessary part of the assessment process.

PREASSESSMENTS FOR GROUPING

Assessments inform daily work. Preassessment, sometimes called pretesting or diagnostic assessment, provides information about a student's understanding of the content about to be studied. The results can eliminate unneeded daily work for some students and show the need for interventions for others. Pretesting informs you when to accelerate and increase depth and complexity, and creates time for ongoing projects that connect content to students' interests.

Pretest to:

■ Assess knowledge of basic skills and new content

■ Create learning groups based on mastery of targeted concepts

■ Compact regular curriculum into shorter time periods

This section describes practical, easy-to-manage strategies for pretesting students. These simple strategies can provide useful information for forming learning groups. Knowing what a learner is bringing to the lesson helps establish strong groups. Placing students with limited knowledge in a group with students who possess a high degree of understanding does not support the learning of either student. We encourage teachers to select one pretesting strategy at a time to use in different contexts. Once you are comfortable using one, you can move on to the next strategy. You will find that some strategies naturally lend themselves to certain subjects and topics that you teach. It is important to note that many of these strategies can be used at multiple points within the lesson structure. Refer to pages 83–86 for a chart that briefly describes all the assessment strategies discussed in the remainder of this chapter.

Strategy: One-Pagers

One-pagers assess student understandings in an open-ended framework. The single blank page can be divided into sections or left as a full blank canvas upon which students demonstrate their understandings. The one-pager allows the student to present both a visual and textual representation of the content.

Classroom Scenario: Elementary

Ms. Andrews uses a one-pager to assess her students' understanding of the Latin stems they are studying. Students randomly select a stem from the list of stems that have been taught. Students are then challenged to individually complete the one-pager demonstrating their understanding. Ms. Andrews' one-pager starts as a blank paper divided into five sections, one rectangle in the center with dividing lines creating an additional four sections. Students place a Latin stem in the center rectangle, in the other four sections students provide a definition, an illustration, a sentence, and other words utilizing the stem. The one-pager can be modified to allow any number of options.

Classroom Scenario: Secondary

"Demonstrate your understanding of the key events that led up to the Boston Massacre. Visually represent the information in a one-pager format with no more than fifteen words," said Mr. Riley to his AP History class. Mr. Riley uses the one-pager to gain his students' understanding prior to beginning the unit of study. Requiring a visual representation of the information challenges his learners to make deeper connections.

Strategy: Concept Maps

Generalizations, theories, and principles are derived from conceptual understandings. Concept maps enable students to demonstrate their depth of knowledge of the content and share their ability to "see the big picture." You might have students create a concept map using specific vocabulary or identified elements. To extend the complexity, remove the scaffolding vocabulary and elements.

Classroom Scenario

In Mrs. Rosen's fifth-grade class, students worked in teams to construct a concept map representing their understanding of family life during the Civil War. Mrs. Rosen added a second component by asking students to represent the role of the teenager during this period. Teams could generate their maps using computer tools or paper and markers. Once teams had constructed their maps, they were given the opportunity to present and share their representations.

Strategy: Empty Outlines

With this strategy, you present incomplete outlines to students to gauge their ability to move from parts to a whole using their knowledge base. The outlines can also be used in formative or summative assessment. The goal is to complete the outline by filling in the missing information, one piece at a time. The task is easily differentiated by increasing or decreasing the amount of missing information. This process may be difficult for a holistic learner as they often do not see the pieces until the whole concept is revealed. Allowing students to see a partial whole and then work in reverse to add the missing components challenges the brain to work in both a divergent and convergent manner.

Strategy: Cubing

Cubing can be used in all disciplines and gives students the opportunity to construct meaning about a given topic in six different ways. The cube may be constructed from paper or made of wood. Each side of the cube asks the student to use a different thinking process:

- Describe It (What is it like?)
- Compare It (What is it similar to or different from?)
- Associate It (What does it make you think of?)
- Analyze It (How is it made or what is it composed of?)
- Apply It (What can you do with it? How is it used?)
- Argue For or Against It (Take a stand, arguing for or against it)

Cube questions serve as a starting point when you want students to analyze or consider various aspects of a topic. Cubes can be an after-reading strategy that requires students to think critically about a topic. When students work with cubes, they apply information in new ways. Cubes can be differentiated by interest and readiness.

Strategy: Top Ten

This tool helps students represent key elements of the topic or unit of study. As the top ten lists are developed, students learn to differentiate between themes, main ideas, and details. You can add more challenge for advanced learners by asking them to prioritize the list and defend their rankings. When students must justify their rankings, the complexity of the task increases significantly. Focusing students on what is important about the topic helps them become more discerning in the learning process.

Classroom Scenario

Mrs. Black began the weather unit by asking her third graders to provide her with the top ten things they know about clouds. She gave her students five minutes. As the students finished, Mrs. Black walked around the room picking up their lists. They varied in complexity from "clouds are white and fluffy" to "stratus clouds are thin." As she approached one of her students, he responded with, "Sorry, Mrs. Black, I was only able to come up with thirty-two things." Another student quickly piped up, "Mrs. Black, I am close to having thirty things about clouds!" What does this diagnostic information tell Mrs. Black? Her students showed three distinctive levels of knowledge: those with very little specific content knowledge, those with some background, and her two students with significant background. Mrs. Black will use a lesson extension with these two students.

Strategy: KWL Charts

A KWL chart stands for: "What do the students already *know*?" "What do the students need and *want* to know?" "What did the students *learn*?" It's an effective preassessment tool as well as a summative evaluation tool to measure the level of understanding at the end of unit. Many teachers use the L part as an open-ended question on an exam, allowing students to share the depth of knowledge they gained during the unit of study. KWL charts can also be used in formative assessment. *Note:* You can make an accommodation for ELL or special needs learners by allowing them to complete the L portion using a graphic organizer.

Strategy: Minute Papers

Minute papers offer students a single minute to share their knowledge on a topic. The emphasis is on the content. A question can be the impetus for the paper or it can be open-ended, offering learners a chance to demonstrate the depth of their understanding. Students can share their thoughts on an index card that you collect and use to help guide group development.

Strategy: Most Difficult First

An initial step toward more formal compacting, this strategy is most effective with skill-based assignments.

- With a new assignment, decide which items represent the most difficult examples of the entire task. They may appear sequentially, near the end of the assignment, or from different sections of the assignment.

- Choose no more than five examples.

- Write the assignment on the board and highlight the most difficult part.

- Those students that attempt the most difficult part first and answer all parts correctly do not have to complete the rest of the assignment.
- Those who do not meet the criteria return to complete the whole assignment.

This strategy permits students to demonstrate mastery more quickly and allows them to move onto more challenging enrichment activities within the same topic of study.

FORMATIVE ASSESSMENTS IN GROUPS

Formative assessments and activities are designed to guide your instruction. They occur *every* day in *every* lesson in a differentiated learning environment. Formative assessment is a dialogue, a quick check, the "yes" uttered when a student connects. Informal formative assessments can help you quickly gauge how well students are grasping the content when learning at different levels of complexity. Then you can strategically target instruction at the students' challenge levels in engaging, student-driven ways that develop complex thinking. Formative assessments allow for the creation of learning groups in a systematic grouping model. The assessments are provided to all students and aligned to the standards and objectives to be assessed. In flexible learning groups, formative assessments help you make the strategic changes within the groupings. Consider how you can use the following tools with your grade level and content.

Strategy: Observational Notes

Observational notes are one of the most valuable tools in a teacher's arsenal of strategies. Watching and listening as students productively struggle through tasks offers insight into the thoughts of the learners, whether working independently or in a group. We gain a great deal of knowledge from watching and listening to our students as they work through the learning process.

Classroom Scenario

Mrs. Miller's first graders are gathered around a table at the back of the classroom. Their excitement is evident, yet they speak in hushed whispers. Three of their caterpillar cocoons have cracked and the butterflies are emerging. The children are enthralled with the process. Mrs. Miller stands at the back of the group, jotting down notes on a simple roster sheet. She notes that Marcus, Rylie, Amanda, and Kyle used scientific vocabulary as they whispered about the process.

Mrs. Miller notes that Ryan has begun figuring out the number of days until they will need to release the butterflies to ensure their survival. Brian has quickly lost interest in the process and is ready to move to the next activity. Kendra and Paul are wondering if the butterfly wings will really have symmetry like the ones they colored in class. These observations tell her a great deal about her students and the next steps that she may want to explore with them as well as the grouping structures she will use for the next day's activities.

Strategy: Exit Tickets

Exit tickets in the form of a single question, a minute paper, or even a muddy moment (see page 73 for details) give you a needed glimpse into students' learning to guide upcoming instruction. This could be as simple as providing each student with an index card prior to leaving class. Pose a question (or a few questions) to gauge students' levels of readiness for the next day. Then sort the cards into three groups that indicate students at similar knowledge levels. These are your groups for the next day.

Strategy: Give Me Five

You can use this strategy individually as well as in a group. For example, Mrs. Cruz asks group members to "Give Me Five," and each student identifies their level of understanding of a topic by displaying one to five fingers at chest-level. Five fingers indicate they feel they have a strong understanding, while one indicates they are struggling significantly with the content and/or activity. As a team, members discuss their understandings and come to a team level of understanding. Following the team discussion, Mrs. Cruz asks each group their "Team Five." This information helps determine which groups Mrs. Cruz will work with the following day.

Strategy: Blue/Yellow/Green Cards

You can use this strategy to quickly group students. As students are working through an activity, place a colored card on their desks. Each color denotes to the teacher a level of understanding. For example, students receiving a blue card may be struggling with the concept, students with a yellow card have a good grasp but need additional practice, and those given a green card have demonstrated that they are ready to move on. The colored cards enable you to quickly put students into flexible groups for additional support or more advanced instruction. Be sure to switch up the card colors each time you use this strategy so that students are less aware of what levels the colors indicate.

Strategy: Muddy Moments

This strategy encourages the student to share exactly where he or she is lost or confused. Learning to identify what you don't understand can be as significant as being able to summarize what you do understand. At times, an oral round robin approach works well, because it allows students to hear where others are confused, as well. Comments such as, "Yes, I am where Anthony is. I don't understand that part either," support students in the learning process. Working as a team to articulate understandings (or lack thereof) provides a supportive learning environment. Muddy moments can also be used as exit tickets. With this approach, you can go through students' "muddy moment" index cards and make appropriate adjustments in the next day's lesson plan. Using muddy moments in a verbal format offers students the chance to engage with the material and their peers. "What frustrates and confuses you about the text? Why?"

Strategy: Five Words

"What five words would you use to describe . . . ? Explain and justify your choices." This assessment strategy offers a quick means of gauging student vocabulary and depth of knowledge on a given topic. Students can be grouped based on their level of understanding of the relationships and factors involved in the content.

Classroom Scenario

When asked to describe the main character in the novel she is reading in her literature group, Alicia chooses the words, "volatile, aggressive, anxious, solitary, and unforgiving." Others in the group agree with her choices, except with the word "solitary." Alicia shares her reasoning behind the choice to the group: "Though Rider was always with groups of people, he failed to let anyone get close to him emotionally; he lived an emotionally solitary existence." The discussion continues as others in the group offer examples. Alicia demonstrated a deep understanding of the character beyond his surface behaviors.

Strategy: Study Guides

Study guides ask students: "What are the main topics, supporting details, important contributions, terms, and definitions related to this topic?" These components guide this formative assessment strategy. They enable you to compact new content by reducing the amount of time students spend learning grade-level standards. Develop the study guide using identified standards and assessment checkpoints. List lesson standards sequentially with designated checkpoints designed to document progress while the student moves through material at a more rapid pace. Whether working independently or in a small group, a study guide helps ensure that a student's level of understanding is maintained.

Collect data at each checkpoint to determine the student's understanding of the material. Students continue with the study guide as long as they are meeting the level of proficiency you have determined. This method increases time spent on extension lessons and allows students who have demonstrated a rapid acquisition of the grade-level material to go more deeply into the content. Study guides may be used with or without an extension menu.

Strategy: Socratic Discussions

The Socratic questioning process challenges students to move beyond their personal perspectives to see the views of others. Preparing students for Socratic discussion requires that they all have an integral knowledge of the content. This student-led discussion increases critical thinking for all. Socratic discussions are an effective way to explore ideas in depth and can be used at all grade levels, ability levels, and at different points within a unit or project. They can be based on an issue, a reading selection, or an aspect of the content in need of deeper understanding.

Using Socratic questioning promotes independent thinking in students and gives them ownership of what they are learning. Higher-level thinking skills are required while students think, discuss, debate, evaluate, and analyze content through their own thinking and the thinking of those around them. These types of questions may take some practice on both your and your students' parts since it may be a whole new approach.

Tips for Socratic discussions:
- Pose significant, probing questions that provide meaning and direction to the dialogue.
- Use wait time; allow at least thirty seconds for students to respond.
- Follow up on students' responses.

- Periodically summarize in writing the key points that have been discussed.
- Draw as many students as possible into the discussion.
- Let students discover knowledge on their own through the probing questions you pose.

Classroom Scenario

Mrs. Andres begins by having her students read, "The Letters from Birmingham Jail" by Dr. Martin Luther King Jr. She challenges them to think about these letters in relation to King's "I Have a Dream" speech. Students generate questions that they will use to drive their discussion. Mrs. Andres divides students into two groups to allow for more student interaction.

Each group begins their discussion with the question posed by Mrs. Andres: "What are the relationships between these two texts?" As the groups discuss, students move beyond the teacher's question and begin to engage with their own questions. Mrs. Andres knows that her role at this point is to observe with only a small degree of facilitation. Students guide this learning activity. Their depth of understanding is evidenced by the questions they generate and responses they provide.

Strategy: SOS Summaries

In this strategy, SOS stands for *statement, opinion,* and *support*. You offer a statement to students, not a question. Ask students to form an opinion based on your statement and then to provide support for their opinion by listing facts, evidence, and examples. Students then prepare a brief summary linking the statement, opinion, and support. This format helps prepare students for document-based questioning activities often found in Advanced Placement coursework. The activity can be extended by having students provide support for the opposing opinion in a clear and concise manner.[1]

Strategy: Quick Write/Draw

A favorite of many teachers, this method is a visual representation with a written explanation that provides a clear picture of student understandings of a topic. Ask students to quickly draw an image to represent an objective or set of objectives and then write how the image is connected to the topic. A quick draw is not an elaborate illustration, rather is it a simple sketch of the ideas related to the topic. The written component is used to enhance and expand upon the sketch created by the student.[2]

Strategy: Textbook/Web Pages

When building a textbook/web page, the student must determine the most significant information on the topic. This requires students to critique, validate, and prioritize information. Once the information has been identified, the student chooses how to represent the information on the page. What is the most logical layout? Would a graphic represent an aspect of the information with more clarity than text? How should vocabulary be identified and addressed? The textbook/web page can be a single assessment tool or one that evolves as students' understandings grow.[3]

1. Dodge, J. (2009). *25 Quick Formative Assessments for a Differentiated Classroom.* New York: Scholastic.
2. Dodge, J. (2009).
3. Dodge, J. (2009).

Strategy: Opinion Charts

For this strategy, students are directed: "List opinions about the content on the left column of a T-chart, and support your opinions in the right column." Having students support their thinking allows you to see their level of understanding and conceptual development along with misconceptions that may inhibit further growth. **Figure 3.7** shows an example.

Figure 3.7 Sample Opinion Chart	
OPINIONS	**SUPPORT**
Animals belong in the wild.	Life expectancies are lower for animals in captivity.
Animals become helpless in zoos.	They lose the ability to hunt.
Animals are lonely in zoos.	They are kept isolated in cages.

Strategy: Yes/No Cards

Students make a card with "Yes" (or "Got it") on one side, and "No" (or "No clue") on the opposite side. Then you ask an introductory or review question. Students who know the answer hold up the "Yes" card, and if they don't know the answer they hold up the "No" card. This is very effective to use when introducing vocabulary words that students need as a knowledge base for a specific unit of study.

Strategy: SAD Corners

With this strategy, students formulate their own views and opinions along a continuum rather than dialectically. Present students with a statement and ask them to determine whether they strongly agree (SA), agree (A), disagree (D), or strongly disagree (SD) with the statement. Then ask them to move to the appropriate corner of the classroom identified with the option they chose. A class discussion follows as students are given the opportunity to outline and defend their positions, refute the arguments of others, and reevaluate their own ideas.

Classroom Scenario

The corners in Ms. Walker's sixth-grade room are numbered: Corner 1 is reserved for those who *strongly agree* with a statement, corner 2 is for those who *agree,* corner 3 is for those who *disagree,* and corner 4 is reserved for those who *strongly disagree* with the statement. The statement Ms. Walker provides is: "War is inevitable." Students move to their chosen corners without comment. Upon arriving, groups are given five minutes to discuss their opinions. A one-time change in location is allowed following the discussion time. Next, students research and prepare to defend their opinions.

Strategy: Quick Checks

Quick checks are a rapid formative assessment technique that can be used daily and/or weekly in any content area and during any lesson. A quick check of five problems or questions gives you an opportunity to gauge the level of understanding of students on a given topic. When using quick checks, be sure that you are addressing a specific set of objectives. Students should be able to complete a quick check in five to ten minutes. Often, teachers use a quick check as an exit ticket (see page 72). Google Forms can be used to create easy quick checks and the results can be seen immediately by students.

Strategy: Whiteboard Checks

A whiteboard check can be used anytime in the learning process. It enables you to see the process the student is using to solve the problems at hand. Notice that it is about showing the *student's* process, not necessarily the teacher's process. The phrase "Show me your process" is key when working with some students who prefer to work out problems in their heads. These students often intuitively combine steps and procedures, solving the problem in a different way from how it was demonstrated in class. Give students a problem to solve and have them represent the procedural steps on their whiteboard along with the answer.

While having the correct answer is important in this type of assessment, it is primarily about the process. When students have completed the problem, they hold up the whiteboard for you to see. A simple thumbs-up to a student can be all that is needed to allow him or her to move on to the next aspect of the activity. If the process is unclear or there are misconceptions, you can redirect the student to, for example, "look at your second step" or have a quick conversation with him or her.

Strategy: Turn and Talk

"Turn and Talk" is another assessment strategy that supports communication and collaboration. Provide a specific topic of conversation for students and listen to their dialogues as they verbalize their ideas and understandings. This provides you valuable information. Through this process, students can challenge each other, expand their understandings, and build on their own knowledge. Some teachers provide a self-assessment following this method to collect additional data.

Strategy: A & E Cards

"A & E" stands for *assessment and evaluation*. With this strategy, students have cards with their names. At the end of class, you ask an overarching question that encompasses the main ideas discussed in class that day. Students jot down their answers and hand you their cards as they walk out the door. You can determine a lot about where your students are with the content based on their answers. Sort the cards into groups based on the level of understanding shown in their answers. The next day, use this information to place students into flexible learning groups for the learning activity you have planned.

Classroom Scenario

Honors teacher, Pamela Ehlert, describes how she modifies and uses the A & E card strategy:

"I have used the A & E card strategy as a kind of exit ticket before, much as the description listed, but I have also used it a little differently. I like using it the way described as long as the student's name is on the opposite side of the card, because it allows me to sort the cards based on student knowledge rather than on my own preconceived ideas of who understands the concept.

"In a slightly different way, I use the strategy as a review activity/exit ticket at the end of a lesson, where I give students a direction, such as 'Give an example of a pronoun, or write a math problem showing one of the properties of addition.' Then, I ask the students to try to find someone else in the room who has the same or similar answer. Students walk around listening to each other's answers while looking for a partner.

"After students are grouped by similar answers, I have them choose a spokesperson to communicate their response to the rest of the class. This serves as a good formative assessment tool for me, as I can tell students' levels of understanding, and they have already pretty much grouped themselves for further practice! I see this being a great pretesting strategy as well, because the kids enjoy the interaction and it gives the teacher a visual of who understands what."[4]

Strategy: Reflective Journals

Reflective journaling is a way to practice writing and thinking. It differs from typical class notes in that it is not a passive record of data/information given. It should not be a mere "listing of events" but rather a student's reflection upon lessons learned and a personal record of an educational experience. Maintaining a journal can serve as a means of communication with the teacher or as a conversation between the content and the learner. Journaling provides the opportunity for regular feedback between student and teacher and is a platform for the synthesis of knowledge and ideas. Journaling also helps develop critical thinking.

Strategy: Word Journals

Vocabulary is a good indicator of student understanding. When students can synthesize information into a single word, the depth of their understanding is revealed. In a word journal, the student, or group of students, is asked to choose a single word that represents the concept, event, or idea. Once the word has been selected, the student or group explains the selection. What elements of the word connect to the concept? Why?

Strategy: Wonder Journals

A wonder journal is a place for students to wonder about the topic under study as well as about topics that simply puzzle them. Giving students permission to wonder can spark creative energy and offer a wealth of possibilities. Students can write or draw items that they wonder about in their journal. Providing students with the chance to share their wonder invites discussion and helps students connect and form interest-based groups.

Strategy: Intrigue Journals

To use this strategy, you might ask students: "List the five most interesting, controversial, or resonant ideas you found in the readings. Include page numbers and a short rationale." Intrigue journals provide an outlet for students' ideas related to a topic of study. You may facilitate the process by offering a guiding question or the students may develop the content on their own. Intrigue journals can also be used with teams of students.

---

4. Pamela Ehlert teaches at Whispering Wind Elementary School in Paradise Valley Unified School District, Arizona. Quoted with permission.

Classroom Scenario

Group work and intrigue journals are hallmarks of Mrs. Williams's history class. She forms groups based on student-demonstrated content knowledge. Each week she presents students with a current event, a short story, a poem, or other text. Students respond individually to the content and then meet as a group to discuss and share their thoughts. Finally, the group writes their response to the text in a collaborative manner. Mrs. Williams's use of intrigue journals supports her students' development of critical and higher-order thinking. By utilizing a collaborative group assignment, she seeks to extend the learning into a real-world construct.

SUMMATIVE ASSESSMENTS IN GROUPS

Summative assessments come in many forms and often represent a high-stakes event for the students and at times for the teacher. Through the formative assessment process, you begin to gauge how your students will perform on a summative assessment. Assessments given at the end of the unit or year determine a student's mastery of a topic after learning has occurred. These include but are not limited to:

- unit exams
- final exams
- projects
- performances
- district and state exams

Information from summative assessments is a valuable grouping tool. Data about the efficacy of certain grouping configurations can help guide your future groupings. For example, if the summative data shows that a student in a particular group did not achieve as expected, you may want to revisit the grouping configuration for the particular student to see if he or she was getting the type of support needed while working within that particular group.

In short, summative assessments offer two valuable benefits to the teaching and learning process. First, they offer a means by which you can gauge the student's mastery of material for a given subject, as we can see in Mrs. Meyer's high school class in the following scenario. Second, they offer the opportunity to look at strategy success or failure over time as shown in the school scenario from Holden Park Elementary on page 80.

Classroom Scenario

Mrs. Meyer's ninth-grade English class takes two final exams and a district benchmark assessment. One final is focused on Latin and Greek roots and vocabulary and a second is a writing assessment. The district exam focuses on the content for the given quarter or semester. These assessments are graded and can be used to determine proficiency levels for the students in the course. Final projects and performances are used in the same manner.

These summative assessments not only show the mastery level of the learner, they can also provide valuable information to Mrs. Meyer about how well material was received. As a teacher, you are constantly seeking to hone your craft and provide a better means of engaging your students with the learning process. Looking at students' final exam data can provide you with information for reflection and refinement of the course material and instructional and grouping methods used.

State assessment data is often unavailable until the following year. So, this data moves with the learner to the next year's teacher. Students demonstrating a lack of proficiency on these assessments may need remedial support structures, just as those demonstrating high levels of proficiency may be candidates for more advanced course work. This data can also be used to help the teacher who was responsible for teaching the content. Once it's available, take time to reflect on the data and adjust your curriculum, instruction, and grouping strategies where needed. All educators must study and respond to the trends and patterns the state assessment data show at the class, grade, school, and even district level, as shown in the following example of Holden Park Elementary.

Classroom Scenario

Early in the fall, the fourth-grade teachers at Holden Park Elementary look closely at their previous year's state assessment data. They are comparing not just one year but looking at math scores over a three-year period. They are excited to see a steady increase in student performance in both the Geometry and Algebraic Thinking strands of the assessment. These were areas of focus of the team's earlier assessment of student proficiencies. The increase in performance indicates that the grouping strategies being implemented were making an impact on student understandings. The three years of data supported this assumption. Being able to look at summative data over a period of time allowed the teachers to assess their strategies in relation to the progression of students.

Assessing Group Work

When *cooperation* is emphasized in group work, tasks lend themselves to a "divide and conquer" approach; students divide the tasks into equal portions. Typically, everybody does their portion, so students work alone. Members feel individual accountability and they never gel. Members submit their finished products to one person who puts it together. Quite often, not everybody delivers similar quality work, and some don't deliver in a timely fashion or at all. Assessment of this type of group work can be difficult since the group may or may not have truly worked as a team.

Collaboration, on the other hand, means working together to create something new in support of a shared vision. The key points are that it is not focused on individual effort, something new is created, and the group is connected by a shared vision. Collaboration does not happen automatically in a group, it requires the intentional creation of a collaborative learning environment.

In our interdependent world, collaboration is the bedrock of creative solutions and innovation. Collaborative group work places students in real-world situations, and the work generated encompasses the energies and knowledge of all participants. Helping students understand the collective power of collaboration is critical. As a group, students have the power to encourage teammates to perform, thus establishing group norms. These norms support all members in fulfilling their roles within the group. Assessment can be focused on the collaborative skills of the group using collaborative rubrics as well as the actual assignment given to the group. When collaboration skills are explicitly taught, students, teachers, and parents can see the value and need for grouping. Learning the strategies and structures that enable learners to collaborate successfully is key to student success. We shared these strategies and additional information on collaboration in chapter 2.

Sharing with Parents

As we've discussed, keeping parents in the learning loop is a necessity in ability grouping structures. It is also a task some teachers need guidance on when grouping students working at different levels or on differentiated work. Increasing complexity using collaborative and flexible working teams is new to many parents; typically, it isn't the way parents were taught. Not only are the varied groupings different, so are the ways in which students are assessed and graded. Supporting parents' understandings of how content is taught and assessed promotes a mutually beneficial relationship among the student, parent, and teacher.

Though some students will opt to work alone when given the option, the benefits of grouping students are extensive. Still, many students' parents are critically aware of anti-grouping sentiments. Teachers frequently hear comments such as these from parents:

"My child does all the work."
"Teams rarely get along."
"Deadlines are difficult to manage."
"Group work lacks focus."
"There is no fair way to grade group work."

Students usually have been taught how to cooperate in a group but not necessarily how to collaborate successfully. All students need experience working in groups because teamwork and collaboration pervade in the real-world work force, and the level of complexity can increase when students bounce ideas off each other.

Parents—and at times, students—struggle with how group work will be assessed when the group formations and the lesson design are not strategically planned, or when there is no individual accountability. If a student lets down the group, the rest of the group has to take up the slack or all students in the group suffer the consequences. Generally, students will take up the slack when a group member fails to complete his or her part, but in doing so, it can engender significant hostility toward the process. To prevent this situation, you need to instate checkpoints and conferences with groups. When you note that group members are not working in a collaborative manner, adjustments to individual student responsibilities and accountability can be made. Keeping parents in the loop with checkpoint data and conference interventions can help maintain a positive learning climate.

In Closing

We began this chapter reminding you that assessment drives instruction and that grades are a manifestation of the assessment process. We provided descriptions of the different types of assessments and examples of how teachers use them to form students' learning groups. We attempted to answer the burning questions that often prevent teachers from allowing students to work in groups or accelerate when needed, including how to assess growth when students are working in different groups, how to know when to use the different types of assessments, and how to communicate progress when students are working at different levels. Finally, we discussed how supporting parents in their understandings of the "how and why" of group assessment helps them appreciate the valuable role groups can play in the differentiation process.

Sample Assessment Strategies

NAME	DESCRIPTION	WHAT TO DO WITH DATA	WHEN TO USE
One-Pagers	Blank page divided into four sections. Allows students to present a visual and textual representation.	Used to assess students' depth of knowledge of the content. Do students have the essential concepts?	Diagnostic Formative Summative
Concept Maps	Focuses on patterns of association. Supports students in making connections and relationships.	Used to discover students' creativity in making connections between concepts. Are learners able to see the big picture as well as the connective details?	Diagnostic Formative
Empty Outlines	Empty or incomplete outlines are presented to the student to complete from their knowledge base.	Used to identify students' recall of information and their ability to organize information into an appropriate structure. Demonstrates how well students are able to recall key pieces of information.	Diagnostic Formative Summative
Cubing	Opportunity to construct meaning six different ways.	Used to see the different thinking processes students are utilizing.	Diagnostic Formative Summative
Top Ten	Students are asked to identify the top ten things known about a given topic.	Quantity and complexity of the responses offer an insight into the level of understanding of the students.	Diagnostic Formative Summative
KWL Charts	K: what do the students already know? W: what do the students need and want to know? L: what did the students learn?	Data supports the teacher in knowing the degree of prior knowledge students possess. It can also be used to demonstrate the knowledge acquired over the course of study.	Diagnostic Summative
Minute Papers	At the end of class students respond to the question: "What is the most important point you learned today?" The goal is to elicit information about student understanding.	Use comments to build learning groups for the next day. Provides issues that need to be focused on for future instruction.	Formative
Most Difficult First	Compacting by assignment, once lesson is taught, the student is given the option of attempting the four or five most difficult problems. If student successfully completes the problems within the given time frame, the student can move on to extension activities or more advanced tasks.	Data enables the teacher to move students forward without requiring unneeded repetitions.	Diagnostic Formative

continued →

Sample Assessment Strategies, continued

NAME	DESCRIPTION	WHAT TO DO WITH DATA	WHEN TO USE
Observational Notes	Notes taken by the teacher throughout the learning process.	This data is invaluable in noting student understandings as well as misunderstandings that might not be seen in a written format.	Formative
Exit Tickets	Can take the form of a single question, a minute paper, or even a muddy moment.	Provides a glimpse into the students' readiness for upcoming content.	Diagnostic Formative
Give Me Five	When asked to "give me five," each student identifies his/her level of understanding of a topic by displaying one to five fingers at chest-level. Five fingers indicate a strong understanding, while one finger indicates significant struggle with the content and/or activity.	Offers a quick visual check of student understanding and provides valuable information for future groupings.	Formative
Blue/Yellow/Green Cards	As students are working through an activity, a colored card is placed on their desks. Colors denote a level of understanding: blue=struggling; yellow=a good grasp but needing additional practice; green=ready to move on.	The colored cards help the teacher quickly place students into flexible groups for additional support or more advanced instruction.	Formative
Muddy Moments	Students respond to the question, "What is the muddiest point for you?" "What was your muddy moment with this content?"	Used to identify misconceptions, conceptual errors, and what concepts are unclear for students. Groups can be formed to move students forward as well as to address material again.	Formative
Five Words	What five words would you use to describe? Explain and justify your choices.	Used to demonstrate students' depth of knowledge in vocabulary as well as their critical and creative thinking in justifying the choices.	Formative Summative
Study Guides	Enables the teacher to compact new content by reducing the amount of time learners spend learning grade-level standards. The guide is developed using the grade-level assessment checkpoints.	Data generated can be used to determine student understanding of new content. Data allows the teacher to observe how rapidly students can acquire information. Students' independence level when learning new content can also be assessed.	Formative

continued →

Sample Assessment Strategies, continued

NAME	DESCRIPTION	WHAT TO DO WITH DATA	WHEN TO USE
Socratic Discussions	Socratic discussions can be based on an issue, a reading selection, or an aspect of the content for which deep understanding is needed. Teacher-facilitated and student-generated questions guide the discussion.	Observational data regarding student participation, preparedness, and level of questions and responses can be used to determine student depth of understanding and ability to make connections within the content.	Formative Summative
SOS Summaries	Statement Opinion Support The teacher offers a statement, not a question. Students give an opinion and provide support for the opinion by listing facts, evidence, and examples. The student prepares a brief summary linking the statement, opinion, and support.	Provides data to demonstrate students' ability to support with facts, evidence, and examples. Demonstrates students' level of understanding based on the complexity of the summary statement developed.	Formative Summative
Quick Write/ Draw	A visual representation with a written explanation providing a clear picture of student understandings.	Provides a visual look into the understandings students have created with regard to the topic.	Diagnostic Formative
Textbook/ Web Pages	Students critique, validate, and prioritize information on the given topic. Once the information has been identified, students choose how they will represent the information on the textbook page.	Use data to establish student understanding related to the key points of the topic as well the information that students feel is significant.	Formative Summative
Opinion Charts	Students list opinions about the content on the left column of a T-chart, and support their opinions in the right column.	Enables the teacher to see the level of support students can provide for their beliefs on a given topic.	Formative Summative
Yes/No Cards	Students use cards with Yes/No on sides to demonstrate whether they know the answer to the question asked.	A quick means of determining students' basic understandings of content, especially vocabulary.	Diagnostic Formative
SAD Corners	When presented with a statement, students determine whether they strongly agree (SA), agree (A), disagree (D), or strongly disagree (SD) with the statement. They move to the corner of the classroom identified with the option chosen.	Discussion that follows the activity provides insights into students' understandings and ability to support those understandings.	Formative Summative
Quick Checks	A rapid assessment consisting of five problems or questions that can be used daily and/or weekly in any content area or lesson.	Enables the teacher to gauge the level of students' understanding of a given topic.	Formative

continued →

Sample Assessment Strategies, continued

NAME	DESCRIPTION	WHAT TO DO WITH DATA	WHEN TO USE
Whiteboard Checks	Opportunity for students to visually show their process.	Enables the teacher to see how students are solving problems.	Diagnostic Formative Summative
Turn and Talk	Students are provided a topic to converse about and can challenge each other, expand their understandings, and build on their own knowledge.	Dialogue exchanges enable the teacher to listen as students verbalize their understandings.	Formative
A & E Cards	Students respond to an overarching question on an index card.	Used to determine depth of student understanding related to the content.	Diagnostic Formative
Reflective Journals	A means of practicing writing and thinking in a metacognitive manner; offers a chance for reflection on lessons learned.	Used to identify student understanding of content and provide a look into students' thought processes.	Formative Summative
Word Journals	Students summarize in a single word the concept and provide a brief paragraph explaining their process and reasoning behind the choice.	Used to demonstrate students' depth of knowledge in vocabulary as well as their creative thinking in summarizing and concept development.	Diagnostic Formative Summative
Wonder Journals	Students share their "wonders" regarding the content to be studied. The depth of student understanding can be determined by the level of question asked.	Data can be used to group students by their interest areas, in addition to identifying the depth of knowledge based on the questions to which students are seeking answers.	Diagnostic Formative
Intrigue Journals	List the five most interesting, controversial, or resonant ideas you found in the readings. Include page #s and a short rationale (100 words).	Used to identify the connections and relationships students are making about particular content. Groups can be made based on the complexity and depth of responses.	Formative

CHAPTER 4
Grouping Support for Administrators, Coordinators, and Teachers

GUIDING QUESTIONS
- How can we embed grouping strategies into our school initiatives?
- What type of support can school administrators and coordinators provide to teachers who use grouping strategies?
- How can we create resources and training to support those teaching different levels of student groups in the same class?

Schools that successfully incorporate grouping methods recognize the importance of providing time to teachers for collaboration and ongoing professional development. In this chapter, we share plans for school and district leaders to prepare and support teachers who flexibly group. We describe how to set up teacher workshops, peer collaboration, and teacher planning meetings, as well as methods for integrating grouping practices into a school or district's existing structure. Also included are methods for accessing and sharing resources. Finally, we discuss proven strategies for providing ongoing teacher support for innovative grouping practices.

Support for Grouping within Administration

School administrators need guidance and support for effectively forming learning groups and supporting teachers. When grouping practices are prevalent throughout a school district, this training should be embedded in other district initiatives. This allows principals to identify ways they can then support the teachers at their sites. Having these conversations at the district level increases the likelihood that principals will have the tools they need to support their teachers in the grouping process.

Classroom Scenario

Mr. Robert Dawson is the principal of Sonoran Sky Elementary School in Scottsdale, Arizona. Mr. Dawson describes how his students are grouped in a variety of ways. Note that he highlights the grouping of his school's large gifted student population in addition to the general population.

"At our school, we group students in several ways. As background information, we have many advanced learners.[1] We follow the district's plan for how to group students. Gifted students are cluster grouped at each grade level, have daily content replacement (for math and reading), and have a self-contained gifted program (for highly gifted students who are radically accelerated). Students are grouped into each of these programs based on their qualifying gifted test scores.

"At the beginning of the year, we outline the expectations of what the flexible grouping will look like during parent night. I schedule an evening parent meeting at the beginning of the school year to help explain how we form our groupings. I also host a morning coffee chat. Flexible grouping and cluster grouping are the main topics we talk about. There can be as many as seventy-five parents at my coffee chats. I also make flexible grouping the topic of one of my beginning-of-the-year newsletters.

"Each grade level varies slightly as to which subjects they flexibly group, but they all flexibly group all students for reading and math. Some switch for science and social studies, as well. This information is all communicated at the beginning of the year. Teachers give Common Formative Assessments for each unit and adjust their flexible groups each time a new unit is addressed.

"Grade levels also vary as to who is the high-level, medium-level, and low-level teacher. Based on student results from the formative assessments, there may be one high level, two middle levels, and one low level, or possibly two highs, one middle, and one low group. With this model, students get exposure to different students and teachers throughout the year with instruction focused at students' challenge levels. I believe this helps students increase the complexity and richness of their experiences here at school.

"I always talk to my teachers about the importance of communication. I provide a common grade-level planning time to support their collaboration. I work with grade levels and teachers to make sure they have a sound, accurate, and timely communication plan. If they communicate well, this eliminates almost all problems.

"School administrators lead hectic lives; from the school principal to the superintendent, administrators continuously juggle numerous pressing responsibilities and demands. Their objective of marshalling people toward a common goal directs their time. Finding time to plan for high-ability students often becomes an administrator's priority only after issues arise. When this occurs, affected parties typically convene to plan interventions to support that particular student and teacher. Even when these interventions are successful, the results do not normally impact other students with similar needs.

"Instead of attempting to solve problems as they arise, it makes more sense to plan proactively. School administrators need to do this for all groups of students. Our goal is to embed the learning needs of high-ability students into all aspects of the school day. By doing so, we bring attention to the needs

---

1. Gifted programs in Arizona require that students score a 97 percent or higher in any one area on a state-approved ability or IQ test: verbal, nonverbal, or quantitative.

of *all* students in *all* planning meetings. We recommend building services for advanced learners into existing school structures and working collaboratively with district administration. Supporting advanced learners then becomes part of the administrators' ongoing marshalling efforts."[2]

COLLABORATION AMONG ADMINISTRATORS

We build understanding and support through relationships and collaboration. Relationship-building among school administrators is critical for supporting grouping practices. When ability grouping, teachers need to learn and implement new approaches toward personalizing learning. These new approaches include using pretesting practices, formative assessments, and associated grouping strategies. The approaches become effective and sustainable when there is a common understanding and district-level support.

Collaboration among administrators who understand the need to advance learners at all levels helps create common practices and sets the stage for supporting teachers. Collaboration among principals and administrators at the district level helps produce shared expectations and build sustainable systems.

To fully obtain the benefits of grouping strategies, school administrators must recognize that students have different and varied learning needs, some of which require more than subject remediation or acceleration. They must also recognize the benefits of flexibly grouping students for specific instruction. With administrative oversight, teachers can better analyze their students' achievement data to help determine groupings. They can then plan their grade level's curriculum and instruction accordingly. (Specific methods for using achievement data to form student groups was discussed in chapter 3.)

Support for Grouping within Districts

In this section, we describe examples of collaboration between departments within a district, with a focus on how these interactions can benefit schools using grouping strategies. Our goal is to demonstrate how integrating the needs of all students— including our struggling learners, ELL students, gifted students, and those in the general population—into all relatable functions of a school district builds support for teachers and students.

COLLABORATION AMONG DEPARTMENTS TO IDENTIFY HIGH POTENTIAL IN DIVERSE POPULATIONS

Consider incorporating actions such as those outlined in the following sections when collaborating with these departments and directors: Language Acquisition, Special Education, Curriculum, Grants, Professional Development, Assessment, and Fine Arts. This collaboration will help identify strengths in diverse populations, which is often a struggle for schools and is necessary in forming flexible learning groups. The

---

2. Robert Dawson is the principal of Sonoran Sky Elementary School in Paradise Valley Unified School District, Arizona. Quoted with permission.

collaboration will also make available resources from other departments that support teachers when instructing in flexibly grouped classrooms.

Language Acquisition Department

Actions and Potential Outcomes:

Train language acquisition testers to recognize signs of mental acuity when administering language testing.

- With training, testers who make initial assessments of a student's language fluency levels will also be able to recognize potential in the students they test. They can then weigh in on which students may require additional attention through remediation, acceleration, and/or enrichment.

Train classroom teachers to recognize high potential in ELL students.

- Virtually all teachers have had preservice training in teaching students with special education and ELL identification, but very few have had preservice training in gifted education. Providing basic training in gifted education to all teachers helps them recognize potential across cultures and ability levels. Indeed, teachers who understand how gifted students think, learn, and behave begin to recognize these signs in students of all cultures, ethnic groups, and socioeconomic levels. Knowing how to recognize strengths in all student subgroups helps teachers know when to form flexible learning groups and reduces the likelihood of relying on stereotypes to form groups, such as assuming the ELL and special education students only need basic skills instruction.

Teach ELL teachers strategies for building critical thinking while also developing language acquisition.

- Some ELL students acquire English much more rapidly than their ELL age peers. When ELL teachers build in higher-order thinking into language development strategies, they can better reach ELL students at different levels.

Group gifted ELL students with non-ELL gifted students whenever possible.

- Being exposed to higher-order thinking skills helps stimulate ELL students' thinking, even among those who are not yet fluent in English.

Special Education Department

Actions and Potential Outcomes:

Provide training in characteristics of giftedness to school psychologists.

- School psychologists often encounter gifted students when testing for special education qualifications, yet many have received very little training in gifted education.

Develop a process for school psychologists to share testing results with your gifted coordinator when they see that a student being tested for special education services scores in the gifted-qualifying range.

- This process helps identify twice-exceptional gifted students and provides important information for classroom teachers. The identification informs teachers that these students will progress more quickly when taught from a strength framework rather than from one of weakness.
- Training school psychologists in gifted education, including identification procedures, characteristics, and programming, lowers the chance of misdiagnoses.

Curriculum Director

Actions and Potential Outcomes:

Build a close relationship with your curriculum director so that he or she can help you access beyond-grade-level curriculum when needed.

- When teachers have access to varied levels of curriculum, they are more likely to use formative assessments, flexibly group students, and provide appropriately advanced instruction.

Use formative and summative assessment data to accelerate curriculum when the evidence demonstrates a need.

- Advanced learners thrive on challenging work and appreciate the opportunity to document mastery.
- Teachers need documentation of mastered skills to confidently accelerate students.

Grants Director

Actions and Potential Outcomes:

Study how title funds can be used to support gifted education in Title I schools. Laws change every few years. Learn the intricacies of what is allowable and discuss the possibilities with your grants director.

- In the 2017–18 school year under ESSA (Every Student Succeeds Act), school districts could use Title I funds to support gifted students in Title I schools or districts. Ideally, this act should help address underrepresentation of gifted students in low income schools.
- ESSA also now allows schools to use Title II funds to provide professional development in gifted education to teachers and administrators. Access to these funds can create or strengthen schools' efforts to build sustainable gifted services.

Professional Development Director

Actions and Potential Outcomes:

Build training in grouping strategies and differentiated instruction into the school or district's overall training plan.

- When teachers see that options are available for training in instructional strategies directed toward advanced learners, they are likely to recognize the importance of seeking the training.

Embed all students' needs into existing training plans and school initiatives.

- Doing so will send the message that teachers need to continually plan for their advanced learners as well as their struggling students in all instructional areas. Teachers will become accustomed to regularly considering these students' different learning needs when planning.

Assessment Director

Actions and Potential Outcomes:

Work closely with your assessment director to obtain and analyze the state and/or district achievement data of all your students.

- With this data you can clearly document areas of strength and need for your students with exceptional needs. Use the data to plan teacher training and areas of curricular focus.

Arrange for grade-level teams to examine achievement data routinely. Teams can examine data during grade-level meetings, in PLCs, and in staff meetings.
- Teachers will use this data to form their flexible learning groups.
- Academic growth for all students becomes an inherent part of daily conversations.

Create a system and time wherein teachers at each grade level can routinely analyze their students' data with assistance from the assessment director.
- Teachers can use the data to discuss grouping and regrouping of students according to need.
- Grade-level teams can then determine how they will level their curriculum and instruction for the different learning groups.

Fine Arts Department

Actions and Potential Outcomes:

Work closely with your district's fine arts coordinator to find out what classes, events, and programs are planned for the year.
- High-ability students are commonly multitalented and enjoy participating in fine arts opportunities. They can build on those experiences when working on projects in the class.
- Art and grade-level teachers may collaborate to plan fine arts lessons that align with class units and projects to increase the depth of students' projects.

Train fine arts teachers on characteristics of gifted students.
- With this understanding, they may recognize signs of gifted and talented students that go unrecognized in an academic setting. They can then modify assignments and share the information with the classroom teacher. This helps classroom teachers recognize students' strengths in areas outside the core curriculum and gives teachers insight into how some nontraditional students learn differently. This information can be useful for forming flexible learning groups.

Preparing and Supporting Teachers Who Group

Teachers commonly report that the primary obstacles preventing them from grouping students is a lack of administrative support and training. In this section, we provide advice on selecting teachers for different learning groups and provide several methods for supporting teachers who use grouping practices. We share suggestions on specific ways to prepare teachers and provide ongoing support systems.

SELECTING TEACHERS FOR DIVERSE LEARNER GROUPS

For effective instruction to take place for diverse learners, teachers must become comfortable with the fluidity inherent in flexible grouping. Diverse learners, as with gifted learners, are often asynchronous in their development. For example, an ELL student may struggle with reading or social studies but be very strong in a nonlanguage-based class such as math.

Teachers must see beyond culture, language, and ability to see the learner that lies beneath the clearly observable traits. Every learner needs to be engaged and challenged to reach his or her potential. Due to the number of different and highly flexible groupings that can occur in a classroom, teachers should also be comfortable with classroom management. The ability to structure learning experiences into small-group formats and then move within the groups to provide instruction is key. When done well, this is truly a sight to behold!

When working with diverse students, many teachers tend to feel that the content needs to be "brought down" to these students' level. However, complexity breeds engagement for *all* learners. When learning experiences lack an appropriate level of complexity, students become disengaged and lose interest in the process. Instructional levels should be high enough so that all students must stretch themselves to grasp the concepts. The teacher can scaffold individual components to a higher or lower degree to address special learning challenges. Teachers in these classrooms seek to be flexible not only in their groupings but in their instructional planning as well.

SELECTING TEACHERS FOR GIFTED-CLUSTER GROUPS

There are several key points to consider when choosing gifted-cluster teachers and teachers who will have groups of advanced learners. First, be sure to give more attention to the necessary skills than to tenure. Don't assume that the teacher with the longest tenure will be the best candidate for teaching a specific group of students. Instead, examine her or his skillset to determine which group would be the best fit.

Teachers who work well with gifted students exhibit most of the following characteristics. They:

- Understand and respect individual differences among students
- Enjoy teaching gifted students and advanced learners
- Have a flexible teaching style in instruction, grading, assessment, and behavior
- Compact and differentiate curriculum regularly
- Demonstrate a balance between whole-group and flexible grouping practices
- Encourage student-directed learning
- Are willing to be questioned and challenged
- Agree to participate in ongoing professional development
- Have effective classroom management skills
- Model lifelong learning to their students

To identify which teachers will be effective using flexible grouping strategies, ask yourself the following questions when observing teachers.

- Is the teacher effectively individualizing instruction to meet the varying needs of students?
- Are students provided opportunities to work at their own pace on assigned class work?

- Are students working together in small groups?
- Does the teacher move around the classroom working with individuals or small groups?
- Are students able to move from one task to another with little direction from the teacher?
- Are students actively engaged in meaningful work?

These are also the signs to look for when doing a teacher observation or evaluation.

DEVELOPING TEACHER LEADERS: ELEMENTARY AND SECONDARY

Teachers helping fellow teachers builds focus and support throughout a school. In such schools, teachers are continually collaborating informally to share lessons and ideas and to trouble shoot. When teachers are purposefully grouping students to best address students' readiness and interest levels, it's helpful to identify specific times when teachers can collaborate. Teachers can discuss grouping criteria and how to make instructional plans that will appropriately challenge all students. During these meetings, teachers can share strategies for moving students from one level to the next and take turns providing examples for developing extension lessons.

Specialists or Lead Teachers

When implementing grouping strategies, designate a teacher leader to arrange planning meetings, share strategies, provide informal workshops, and collect resources. Select someone who has experience in all areas of special needs or at least a willingness to pursue training in the field. Some schools/districts make this assignment a formal position or duty and pay a stipend in addition to the teacher's regular salary. Identifying a lead teacher to be a liaison or specialist at each school builds a system of support and collaboration when ability grouping.

Sample duties might include:

- Attending district-level after-school meetings/trainings
- Reviewing the school's achievement data with teachers to make sure students are appropriately identified and placed
- Identifying students who may be struggling academically and working with their teachers or parents
- Reviewing the characteristics and learning needs of special needs students with the staff and administration in small groups
- Providing or arranging training on instructional strategies for advanced learners

While most secondary schools group students according to course level (such as remedial, grade level, or Honors and AP classes), even within these groupings teachers can have a broad range of learners. All teachers can employ flexible grouping practices to better target instruction. Understanding how all students learn, process information, and make connections can impact how the teacher provides instruction and ultimately improve instruction for all students.

IMPACTS OF GROUPING ON TEACHER EVALUATION

In chapter 2, we described methods for managing a class where flexible groupings were the norm. We discussed topics such as noise, movement, and managing materials. This speaks directly to why some teachers resist group work; they prefer (or believe their principals prefer) to see students working quietly. Engaged students are busy and excited about their learning, which does not always make for a quiet classroom.

When a principal enters a classroom and sees students enthusiastically engaged, he or she can tell that real learning is happening. As a teacher, show your students how to share information with visitors who enter the room during group work. Students within the groups can take turns being the spokesperson for the group. Using this practice, students develop skills in organizing and presenting information, such as describing the purpose of the lesson and the process students are using in their groups.

As a staff member (teacher, coach, coordinator, principal), or whomever else is in a position to do so, you might select a walk-through focus topic for each month or quarter. Teachers can identify one main skill, strategy, or procedure to focus on during this time. It could be one of the strategies discussed in this book, such as pretesting, regrouping students, or using a classroom management procedure. Teachers will demonstrate this strategy for the principal during an informal observation or walk-through. A new skill to practice is chosen for the next month. This helps teachers understand that mastering these strategies may take time and practice and that the administrator supports their efforts.

Designing Professional Development for Grouping Practices

Decisions about professional training should be based on students' achievement data and input from teachers. Creating workshops to help teachers design tiered lessons supports those using flexible grouping methods. For example, in the workshop, teachers could work on modifying lessons in a newly adopted reading curriculum for advanced and diverse learners. In addition to providing training on lesson design and differentiated instruction, schools should provide workshops on various topics pertaining to students' learning needs and methods for teaching them.

Suggested workshop topics:
- Teaching diverse learners
- Social and emotional needs of diverse students
- Pretesting and formative assessments
- Using the results of formative assessments
- Flexible grouping
- Designing lessons tiered to depth-of-knowledge (DOK) levels
- Incorporating critical thinking
- Teaching with depth and complexity

- Grading practices when teaching at multiple levels
- Parent communication when flexibly grouping students

"TEN-MINUTE TIPS"

Use the suggested workshop topics as "Ten-Minute Tips." At each staff meeting, allow ten minutes for a teacher leader to briefly address a specific topic. This keeps teachers constantly thinking about how to incorporate new ideas into their teaching repertoires. It might also get teachers interested in coming to a full workshop on the topic.

AFTER-SCHOOL WORKSHOPS

Providing teacher training at the school can have a strong impact on the instructional practices of your entire staff. This type of training can take many forms. Consider the following:

- Schedule informal site-based workshops following a formal school or district training. Identify components of the formal training that will help teachers implement school or district initiatives.

- Identify specific strategies that skilled teachers on staff possess. These might include strategies that help teachers pretest, form flexible learning groups, create tiered lesson activities, develop and use rubrics, develop critical thinking, or integrate technology.

- Determine informal, site-based training needs by asking grade-level teams to generate topics. Provide a list of training examples with brief descriptions, and let the teacher teams identify which topics might be most useful for their group. For example, Utilizing Formative Assessments: Learn and practice using pretests to form flexible learning groups.

- Schedule after-school, site-based trainings once per month. For example, the first Tuesday of each month. Doing so will encourage teachers to routinely schedule time for these nonobligatory trainings.

- Arrange to provide teachers with clock hours that apply toward recertification or professional growth.

- Identify a teacher leader at each school who would be helpful to your staff and support him or her in receiving the specific professional development needed for your school.

Sample After-School Workshops

The following are a sampling of after-school workshops we offer to our teachers. (The descriptions are ones we've created to appeal to teachers.) Some of the workshops focus on students' diverse learning needs, using formative assessments, and classroom management, while most of the workshops describe teaching strategies that build depth and complexity for students at all levels. Sample workshops include the following.

Meeting the Social and Emotional Needs of Diverse Students
Students are much more than test scores and grades. In this workshop, you will examine the unique social and emotional needs of diverse students, such as

perfectionism, feelings of anxiety, underachievement, and other issues commonly experienced by these students. You will learn methods for creating a supportive environment that encourages social and emotional growth through easy-to-use strategies, guided discussions, and classroom-tested activities.

Explore STEM

This workshop will explore all aspects of STEM and provide ideas for enriching and engaging experiences in any classroom. The focus is on integrating real-world problem-solving, critical thinking, communication, and collaboration through scenarios and hands-on labs.

Inquiring Minds Want to Know! Teach for Questions, Not Answers

Meaningful and relevant questions motivate students to think critically and creatively. In this workshop, you will learn strategies and questioning techniques that empower students to delve deeper into their learning and create an environment for authentic critical thinking.

Socratic Seminar: A Community of Inquiry in Your Classroom

Socratic seminars are suited for any grade level and any subject area. These seminars create a community of inquiry and help students develop critical thinking skills. During this class, you will learn how to create rich dialogue in your classroom using Socratic seminars. We will review the four elements of a Socratic seminar: the text, the question, the leader, and the participants. Most importantly, we will distinguish the difference between dialogue and debate. Then we will engage in a Socratic seminar!

Increase Rigor with Depth and Complexity: Use Content Imperatives!

Learn the essential elements of depth and complexity as identified by Sandra Kaplan. See "Understanding Depth and Complexity" at envisiongifted.com/services/under standing-depth-complexity. Learn how to use content imperatives to structure the learning environment. These thinking tools are designed to enable students to dig deeper in content. They provide a simple way to differentiate and increase complexity.

Cluster Within Your Cluster:
Teaching Strategies for the Cluster Classroom

Bring out the best in all your students! Effective teaching in a gifted-cluster class requires providing many varied opportunities for all students to work at their challenge levels and monitoring their progress. Use ongoing formative and summative assessments to find the unique strengths among your students and cluster them to achieve.

The Schoolwide Cluster Grouping Model: An Introduction

This workshop provides an overview of the Schoolwide Cluster Grouping Model (SCGM) and highlights instructional strategies for adapting regular classroom curriculum and activities to meet the learning needs of high-ability learners. You will learn methods for organizing and managing the gifted-cluster classroom, how to make student class placements, and differentiation strategies to use with all students.

Teaching 21st Century Skills

Twenty-first century skills are the means through which students gather, develop, and utilize information. Embedding these skills and learning outcomes into daily instructional strategies is the challenge this workshop will focus on. Bring the skills of communication, collaboration, creativity, critical thinking, and problem-solving into your lessons.

Document-Based Questions with Google Apps for Education

Does fictional text dominate your curriculum? Learn a great way to infuse your reading instruction with document-based lessons and use Google Applications for Education. This workshop will introduce you to these questions, a motivating and easy way to bring nonfiction to life in your classroom. Don't miss this chance to learn how to use primary and secondary source documents and promote higher-level critical thinking skills.

Pop Culture in the Classroom? Absolutely!

You will learn practical ways to incorporate popular culture (including music, television, and movies) into lessons to better differentiate for today's students. Bring "today" into your classroom!

Differentiation and Project-Based Learning with Math

Use student-generated projects to differentiate in your math classroom. Provide direction and guidance, but let the students create the final products. Examples of math games, slideshows, posters, comic strips, and other projects will be provided, as well as technology-based projects for laptop or tablet users.

SHARING AND ACCESSING RESOURCES

Supporting teachers from multiple sites often proves to be quite the challenge. Yet providing teachers with resources and training is critical to their effectiveness when teaching groups of students at different levels. To accomplish this goal in our school district, we created a digital instructional resource site for our teachers using free Google tools, described in the following section. This resource site has helped us build a collaborative approach that brings resources and support to teachers at every site any time of the day.

Learners Instructional Resource Site

To effectively reach, teach, and assess all students, teachers need resources, guidance, and communication at their fingertips. We created the Learners Instructional Resource Site precisely for this purpose. To support all district teachers, this rich repository provides a wealth of differentiated curriculum and instructional strategies, tools to help teachers document achievement for students working at and above grade level, and numerous teacher training resources. The site provides web-based training, a method for sharing curriculum throughout the district, differentiated lesson plans, and digital resources that include videos of classroom demonstrations, examples of student-produced work, and videos of flexible grouping options.

This dynamic support site keeps current with continual updates. Finding time to plan and learn new strategies are the most common challenges teachers face when attempting to differentiate curriculum and instruction. We have developed this user-friendly site to respond to these hurdles. We organized the resources by creating tabs and links that a busy teacher can quickly access and easily maneuver between, depending on her or his needs. The resource site continually expands as teachers use and contribute lessons and suggestions that increase and enhance its resources.

The major categories on the site include professional development, curriculum development, instructional strategies, achievement documentation, program administration, and communication. In the following lists, we outline a few of the resources included in each section of the resource site that applies to teachers using grouping methods in their schools and classrooms.

Professional Development

- Online workshops
- Videos of instructional strategies
- Workshop presentations
- Digital resources

Teachers can view clips of instructional strategies, see presentations of past workshops, quickly access web-based tips, and obtain district credit for online workshops.

Curriculum

- Language arts: scope and sequence, literary elements, essential maps, grammar/vocabulary plans, schedules
- Mathematics: scope and sequence, essential maps, plans, lessons and projects, curriculum schedules, formative and summative assessment schedules, documentation forms, procedures
- Lesson extensions in core content areas for teachers K–12
- Common Core standards

Instruction

- Repository of differentiated lesson plans, by grade level and content area
- Lessons, plans, and resources for differentiating digitally
- Differentiated instruction objectives

Strategies and methods shared through the site are considered best practices and therefore benefit all learners. Most teachers attending our workshops and adding lessons to the site work with the general student population. These teachers recognize that good teaching is just that: good teaching, which entails instructional strategies that can be modified for any learner. In all classrooms, the population is varied, and differentiation is essential if teachers are to meet the needs of all learners.

At the Learners Instructional Resource Site, teachers can access dozens of differentiated lessons organized by grade level and content area. Each grade level (K–12) has a folder containing lessons categorized by the four major content areas: math, language arts, social studies, and science. Access to lessons at multiple grade levels supports teachers who encourage students to work at their individual challenge levels. Most of the lessons have been created by teachers in our workshops, and therefore are aligned to our state standards and use our district curriculum and resources.

Classroom Scenario

Mrs. Walker is a third-grade ELD (English language development) teacher at a Title I school. She wondered if the strategies shared in her content-based questioning workshop would be of benefit for her learners. Nonfiction text was a challenge for them and she was looking for ways to support their learning. She came away from the workshop with ideas and strategies that she could use the very next day. Mrs. Walker continues to participate in the workshops offered through her district's instructional resource site. When asked by colleagues why she chooses to take these specific workshops, her answer is simple, "Best practices work for all learners, and my room is filled with students who want to learn."

These workshops can take place face-to-face or online. Teachers can take these online workshops anytime outside of school hours for credit that applies toward advancement on the salary schedule. Teachers can also receive additional credit hours by contributing a resource to the Learners Instructional Resource Site after completing an online workshop. These resources might include a lesson plan, a rubric, or a parent letter. Teachers enjoy using the contents of the site individually, with others at their school, and to collaborate across the district. They collaborate via technology using video phones, video chats, screen sharing, telepresence, or blogs, and they greatly appreciate the support for teaching and managing their student groups.

SHARING WITH PARENTS

As noted previously, sharing information with parents is critical for gaining support for grouping strategies. You need to be able to explain the following to parents:

- Why and how you group students; what criteria you use
- How you monitor and document growth
- How you use formative and summative assessments
- How you grade students

In Closing

In this chapter, we stressed the importance of embedding grouping strategies into school- and district-wide initiatives. We emphasized methods for integrating grouping strategies into all aspects of your schools and at the district level. The methods described reinforce the need for administrative support. We shared advice for staffing and developing teacher leaders. And to aid your ongoing efforts to support grouping methods at your school or district, we outlined methods for training teachers, teacher leaders, and school and district administrators.

PART TWO

Instructional Strategies for Flexible Learning Groups

CHAPTER 5
Strategies for Extending Learning Processes in Groups

GUIDING QUESTIONS

- How do I create structures in my classroom wherein groups of students are working on projects that challenge them at their learning levels?

- What role can questioning strategies play in a classroom where students are working at varying levels?

- How can I facilitate learning in a way that all my students will think critically and embrace rigor?

In this chapter, we address seven foundational instructional strategies that extend learning for students who have mastered content prior to instruction, those who can master content more quickly than the rest of the class, and those who need additional support in mastering the content. These strategies focus on complexity, depth of knowledge, personalized learning, multiple intelligences, project-based learning, active questioning, and self-reflective learning. We will demonstrate how the strategies included here can be used effectively with students of all abilities. For contextual understanding, some of the strategies will include scenarios that highlight how the strategies were used in a particular classroom learning setting.

SCAFFOLD INSTRUCTION TO EXTEND LEARNING FOR ALL

Scaffolding both instruction and the learning tasks allows students to engage in learning tailored to their needs. What is scaffolding? From an instructional perspective, scaffolding is providing the appropriate degree of support to promote learning. Supports could include the use of varied resources, the introduction of a challenging or compelling task, or even the use of templates or guides to provide the learner with additional support. Scaffolding is used for all students. Learners struggling with content may require scaffolding that helps decrease the level of complexity of the given task. For example, a teacher may provide a template for students to complete or a study guide that focuses their learning on relevant information. Additionally, advanced learners may need an increase in the level of complexity. These learners could be given multiple templates to choose from or asked to create an organizational structure of their own. Both types of students need a form of scaffolding to ensure that the learning experience meets the level of their needs.

Teachers have endless possibilities, both planned and unplanned, for extending students' thinking. Validating students' previous learning through preassessments opens the door to move learning to the next level. To that end, you can add depth and complexity to all lessons by using foundational strategies such as those described here. In this chapter, we explore strategies for pushing *all* students out of their comfort zones and challenging them to extend and expand their thinking. We present these methods within the context of a variety of classroom grouping structures.

Strategy 1: Make It *Complex*, Not Complicated

When attempting to engage and challenge students, we need to first distinguish between what is *more work*, what is *complicated work*, and what is *complex work*. Unfortunately, common practice for some teachers is to provide students with *more* of the same type of work after they complete the regular assignment. This is neither challenging nor fair to the student. Likewise, sometimes we believe we are challenging our students if we assign *complicated* work. By *complicated*, we mean work that may have a difficult set of steps for students to follow but that does not require any critical thinking or problem-solving. Learners find this type of work tedious. We must ask ourselves if we are assigning work that is more *complicated* or that is truly complex.

"Consider," writes Larry Cuban, "how sending a rocket to the moon and raising a child are both considered difficult, but for different reasons. When you send a rocket to the moon you have to follow a long list of detailed procedures. If you follow them carefully, you can reliably repeat that procedure with a high probability of success. There is no such thing for parenting! Even if you expertly raised one child and wrote down everything you did, following that same set of procedures carefully for the next child does not ensure a high probability of success. There are so many interwoven factors with raising a child that no set of instructions can guarantee success. Accordingly, sending a rocket to the moon is a *complicated* process, whereas raising a child is *complex*."[1]

This example shows how complexity of thought requires choice and direction in the learning. You can't ever completely know how backgrounds, ideas, and strengths influence each student. Therefore, you cannot assume that the lesson you design will address the complex thought processes of each of your students. Building complexity requires student involvement.

THE CONTINUUM OF COMPLEXITY

The Continuum of Complexity (**figure 5.1**) is a tool that adjusts the levels of task complexity for students while maintaining similar content. This process is beneficial when working with the whole class or with small groups on a given topic. The continuum identifies ten areas where instructional adjustments can be made. You can adjust the level of complexity within a given content area or within several areas depending on your objective.

Increasing complexity is a "brain boosting" activity for students. Rather than tiring the learner with tasks that are simply harder to complete (complicated), tasks that are more complex engage students in critical and creative thinking processes.

1. Cuban, L. (June 8, 2010). "The Difference Between 'Complicated' and 'Complex' Matters." larrycuban.wordpress.com/2010/06/08/the-difference-between-complicated-and-complex-matters.

Motivation increases when highly capable students work to complete complex and rigorous tasks. Rigor does not come from the curriculum or content being taught; it comes from what students are asked to do with that content. The tasks you design determine the level of complexity that each learner receives and hence, the level of rigor required to complete them. Rigor and complexity go hand in hand.

Developed by Bertie Kingore, the Continuum of Complexity has you refine lessons within the varied areas identified in the chart. In each of the ten categories, complexity can be increased to intensify the rigor for any student. Using this method, you can clearly identify which students are ready for different levels of complexity at different times. Grouping students by the degree of task complexity differentiates the learning process based on students' immediate learning needs within that specific content.

The tasks in the Continuum of Complexity are listed in a hierarchy with the most basic task at the top and the most complex task at the bottom.

Figure 5.1 The Continuum of Complexity[2]	
Area of Complexity	**Increasing Levels of Complexity**
Degree of Assistance and Support	■ Teacher directs instruction ■ Teacher facilitates instruction ■ Peer assistance ■ Autonomous and independent
Degree of Structure	■ Templates and organizers provided ■ Parameters detailed and prescribed ■ Parameters open-ended ■ Students create structure
Rate of Instructional Pacing	■ Slower with multiple examples ■ Repetition and practice at grade level ■ Minimal repetition and practice ■ Accelerated learning rate
Concrete to More Abstract	■ Hands-on learning; manipulatives provided ■ Teacher provides open-ended organizers ■ Deductive and inductive reasoning ■ Abstract thinking and interpretation required ■ Metaphorical thinking and symbolism
Quantity of Resources	■ Teacher provides single resource ■ Student accesses single resource ■ Teacher provides multiple resources ■ Student accesses multiple resources
Background Knowledge and Skills	■ Teacher provides avenues to build background knowledge ■ Basic understanding is evident ■ Understanding is at grade level ■ Extensive knowledge base ■ Beyond-grade-level expertise needed

continued →

2. Kingore, B. (2004). *Differentiation: Simplified, Realistic, and Effective.* Austin, TX: Professional Associates Publishing. Adapted with permission.

Figure 5.1 The Continuum of Complexity,[2] continued	
Area of Complexity	**Increasing Levels of Complexity**
Complexity of Resources	■ Below-grade-level readability ■ Grade-level resources provided ■ Above-grade-level readability ■ Content is dense with complex vocabulary ■ Application of technology and academic vocabulary
Complexity of Process	■ Well-known and practiced process used ■ Process is less practiced and has few steps ■ Task is short-term, completed in a single session ■ Requires simple research skills ■ Task is long-term with extended time on task ■ Process presents a new experience when multiple steps are added ■ Advanced research skills and independent work behaviors required
Complexity of Product	■ Single answer, fill-in-the-blank format ■ Typical, well-known product required ■ Integrates grade-level skills and concepts ■ New product with structured parameters ■ Open-ended and unspecified parameters ■ Complex with integrated advanced skills and concepts
Complexity of Thinking Skills	■ Memorization or repetition required ■ Comprehension and understanding required ■ Application and analysis are required ■ Synthesis, evaluation, and creativity required

In this next section, we provide descriptions and a few examples of these modifications in action. The examples demonstrate just some of the many ways teachers can increase the level of complexity within each area of the continuum. You will see that even small changes in complexity can have significant impact on the rigor involved in completing the task.

Degree of Assistance and Support

Teacher directs instruction. The teacher provides direct, purposeful instruction to a whole class or small group of students. At this level, the teacher is directing the learning environment. Instruction may be in a lecture format or presentation, but the teacher is the sole provider of information.

Teacher facilitates instruction. In a facilitative role, the teacher guides the instruction through questioning strategies.

Peer assistance. Students are engaged while learning in a small group or partner format. In this framework, students support each other in the learning process.

Autonomous and independent. The highest degree of complexity is achieved when students work independently to process and acquire new information.

In each of these modifications, students work in groups that vary in the degree of support provided by the teacher. Creating groups this way enables you to design learning activities that equip all students with what they need.

Degree of Structure

Templates and organizers provided. The teacher provides the template or graphic organizer that the student will use. This represents the lowest degree of complexity.

Parameters detailed and prescribed. Informational parameters are provided for the student, such as specific headings and categories. When a student develops the organizational structure they will use for the activity, the complexity is increased.

Parameters open-ended. Offering the learner multiple templates or organizers to select from expands complexity. Complexity also increases when students are required to determine the headings, categories, and organizational structures on their own.

Students create structure. Giving the student the responsibility of choosing which template or graphic organizer they will use or designing a template of their own offers the highest degree of complexity of structure.

Adjusting the complexity of structure gives all students the opportunity to use graphic organizers at the level of complexity they need.

Grouping students strategically places them in situations where they can collaborate while engaged in productive struggle. The setting allows students to direct their own learning when making decisions about how to organize and present material. This places their learning in an active and real-world scenario.

Classroom Scenario

In Mrs. Parker's sixth-grade science class, students are working to categorize cell components and their functions. Mrs. Parker is differentiating instruction using the degree of structure component of the Continuum of Complexity. Students in Mrs. Parker's class are placed into four groups based on previous learning experiences and levels of expertise in using graphic organizers. The task remains the same for all groups; what varies is how students will complete the task. Group one, students with the least experience, has been provided a graphic organizer complete with headings. Group two has been given the same organizer but the headings are not provided. It is up to the student to determine what headings are needed. Group three has been offered a choice of three different organizers. These students must select the organizer they feel will best represent the information they have been working with. Students in group four have been asked to create an organizer that represents the data in a clear and concise manner.

All of Mrs. Parker's students are working with the same information but their tasks vary significantly in complexity based on how they will identify and manipulate the information. Mrs. Parker's role is that of facilitator. She monitors students as they identify and then categorize their information. She uses high-level questioning strategies to push students to explore different avenues of thought about the information as well as their choices of organizational structure.

Rate of Instructional Pacing

Slower with multiple examples. The teacher works through examples with the students offering multiple opportunities for students to work with the content.

Repetition and practice at grade level. The teacher provides activities to the student that require repeated practice of skills without direct teacher support, which increases the degree of complexity.

Minimal repetition and practice. The teacher limits the amount of repetition based on the student's ability to master content at an increased pace, thus raising the complexity.

Accelerated learning rate. The student experiences the opportunity to "pace out" of the instructional examples.

Classroom Scenario

Mr. Adams understands that many of his high-ability learners need opportunity to increase the pacing of instruction; they do not need multiple examples to understand the material. To accommodate these learners, he developed a signal that allows students to alert him when they are ready to move from instructional examples to small-group or independent practice. Students needing few examples are offered the opportunity to "pace out" of further examples and move into more independent learning opportunities.

Students move from the instructional arena to other learning opportunities in a fluid manner. For example, Anthony, Lupita, and Jazmine have listened to Mr. Adams as he explained the process involved in completing the task for the day. They participated in the completion of two examples and are now ready to move on to their assignment, while others in the class continue with additional examples. The three students give a signal to Mr. Adams who responds with a nod, releasing them from additional examples they do not need. This process also ensures that learners needing additional instruction and examples do not have their learning interrupted.

Concrete to More Abstract

Hands-on learning; manipulatives provided. Materials provided to the student lets the learner "touch and feel" the learning.

Teacher provides open-ended organizers. The students use organizers and graphic representations to extend their learning.

Deductive and inductive reasoning. Students foster reasoning skills by taking inductive steps to draw conclusions and make inferences.

Abstract thinking and interpretation required. Moving up in complexity to abstract thinking challenges learners to step out of their comfort zones, beyond what they can see and touch.

Metaphorical thinking and symbolism. Students develop a personal connection to the learning process as thinking moves to a metaphorical level. They can symbolize their learning in new and novel ways.

Moving from concrete to abstract learning begins in the primary grades. We see this, for example, as students transition from unifix cubes, to visual representations, to the creation of their own symbolic representations.

Classroom Scenario

Mr. Meyers's classroom poses unique challenges due to the range of abilities and developmental skills. During math time, he increases the complexity for several of his math groups. Students are working on adding two-digit numbers with and without regrouping. Mr. Meyers moves his students into their math rotations. Some students will continue to use their unifix unit cubes to manipulate the problems and demonstrate their understanding. In one of the groups, he has students use a visual representation of the manipulative rather than the actual object. This simple change increases the complexity of the learning experience.

Mr. Meyers's most advanced students have been doing well with the visual representations. Today he asks them to demonstrate their understandings using an open-ended organizer. This requires students to make their own visualization of the information they need to represent. By moving his students from a concrete format to one that is even slightly more complex, he offers additional rigor and challenge.

Quantity of Resources

Teacher provides single resource. The teacher provides students with the resource to be used.

Student accesses single resource. Students are responsible for obtaining a resource. The resource may be one provided by the teacher in which students must determine what specific material to use.

Teacher provides multiple resources. Providing the student with multiple resources significantly increases the complexity of the task. Students must determine which resource to obtain the information from and prioritize the information in the process.

Student accesses multiple resources. When the student is responsible for accessing resources from several sources, they are placed in the role of evaluating information and validating the sources.

Classroom Scenario

Students entering Mrs. Tige's classroom moved quickly to their assigned groups. One group of students is working with the assigned textbook for the class. The directions instruct students to use the information from chapters 5 and 6 to complete the assigned activity. The second group is treated to a basket of books and instructed to use those resources to complete the activity. The third group of students is given the activity and instructed to locate materials that they think will provide the needed information. Students have access to technology along with resources from the school media center. Simply by varying the type and quantity of resources, Mrs. Tige can challenge all her students while they work on the same lesson.

Background Knowledge and Skills

Teacher provides avenues to build background knowledge. The teacher provides information to build background knowledge needed for the student to fully understand the content.

Basic understanding is evident. Students possess a minimal level of understanding. The teacher needs to deepen student background knowledge in specific areas.

Understanding is at grade level. Complexity increases through small-group activities that explore the content.

Extensive knowledge base. Open-ended activities for students with an extensive knowledge base help them stay engaged and view the content through varied lenses.

Beyond-grade-level expertise needed. The task complexity is extended or accelerated due to the complexity of the resources and learning processes the students are engaged in.

Classroom Scenario

Mrs. Banks's students Nathan and Andrew know as much about cloud structures as some college meteorology students. She recognizes that the classroom activities designed for her two other learning groups will not meet the complexity demands for these two students. Building on their intense interest in weather phenomenon, Mrs. Banks asks each boy to create a project demonstrating how a particular weather event impacted a social structure and elements related to that structure. They excitedly begin working together to formulate their plans. In collaborating, their projects take on a life of their own!

Complexity of Resources

Below-grade-level readability. Lowering the readability of a text decreases complexity. However, this can be of value when a teacher is teaching a new skill and does not want students to struggle while reading the text.

Grade-level resources provided. The focus remains on the task at hand and the use of the resources.

Above-grade-level readability. Increasing the readability of resources steps up the level of complexity.

Content is dense with complex vocabulary. Increasing the vocabulary and content density increases the complexity for the learner. When students must navigate both content and vocabulary, the level of challenge is heightened.

Application of technology and academic vocabulary. Increasing the complexity of academic vocabulary within applied technology raises the complexity to its highest level in this area.

Classroom Scenario

Mrs. Jones's students are a diverse group. She has several high-achieving students as well as a small group of struggling learners. The class begins work on a polar animal research report. With the whole class, Mrs. Jones models the use of a tree map as a graphic organizer for collecting information. Students select the animal they wish to research and are ready to begin. Having previously identified the reading levels of her students through diagnostic testing, Mrs. Jones adjusts task complexity for her students by adjusting the complexity of resources made available to them.

Mrs. Jones gives each student a tree map with the basic headings of *Habitat, Food, Predators,* and *Interesting Facts.* She then groups her students by reading level and provides materials so they can practice their research skills as independently as possible. Her lowest-level readers work with text that is at or slightly below grade level yet still provides the necessary content information. She gives her skilled and advanced readers above-grade-level text to increase the complexity of the research task for them. Mrs. Jones has one student with an extremely high reading level and advanced knowledge of animals. To accommodate this student, she provides text with content dense vocabulary and an advanced reading level. She further differentiates the assignment by adjusting the complexity of resources as needed.

As students begin their research, Mrs. Jones facilitates the process by walking among the students and asking them questions to guide them. All her students are engaged in the research process with the same topic. Using the Continuum of Complexity, she has differentiated the learning and increased the challenge for her students.

Complexity of Process

Well-known and practiced process used. The more practice students need with a process, the lower the complexity.

Process is less practiced and has few steps. Limiting the steps required to complete a less-practiced process creates an increase in complexity.

Task is short-term, completed in single session. Single setting tasks are building blocks on the complexity scale. They help the learner strengthen strategies within a single time frame.

Requires simple research skills. Engaging learners in the research process increases the steps and accelerates the time frame involved in completing the task.

Task is long-term with extended time on task. Placing students in situations where long-range planning is required to accomplish the learning task increases the challenge level.

Process presents a new experience when multiple steps are added. Incorporating multistep processes increases the complexity of a known process.

Advanced research skills and independent work behaviors required.
Independent work with a research-based process places the degree of complexity at its highest level.

Manipulating the degree of complexity through process maximizes learning for all students. The initial learning phase within any process is at a basic level of complexity. As the learner works with a process over time, the complexity decreases, so it is important to find ways to maintain the degree of complexity to ensure that students remain engaged in the process.

Classroom Scenario

In Mr. Martin's class, fourth-grade students learn to summarize information with accuracy and clarity. The initial learning process is filled with complexity due to the components involved in the summarization process. Over the course of the year, Mr. Martin discovers that his students have evolved into two different learning groups related to their abilities as they summarize material. To keep students engaged in the learning process, he groups his students into two groups.

Group one continues to work on the initial process framework. Group two has demonstrated mastery of the process, so they can add another dimension to their work. The task becomes a "money summary."[3] The students each have $2.00 to begin. Every word used in the summary costs $0.05. The words "a," "an," and "the" are free. Students are challenged to write a summary getting as close to the $2.00 limit as possible without going over. This new dimension increases the complexity of Mr. Martin's practiced process and provides the engagement his fourth graders need.

Complexity of Product

Single answer, fill-in-the-blank format. The key word here is *single*. There is just one correct response with limited complexity.

Typical, well-known product required. Well-known products typically rely upon well-practiced processes, which result in limited complexity within this framework.

Integrates grade-level skills and concepts. Incorporating multiple skills into the learning process enables students to demonstrate their ability to connect and apply the knowledge.

New product with structured parameters. The creation of a new product significantly increases the complexity and thus the rigor of the task.

Open-ended and unspecified parameters. Opening product parameters to expand the options pushes the learner into more complex learning processes.

Complex with integrated advanced skills and concepts. At this level, the complexity of the process is increased through integrating skills and content.

Increasing complexity through different products incorporates skills learned while promoting creative thinking. Complexity increases rapidly when learners can work outside the parameters you identify.

---

3. Auman, M. (2015). *Step Up to Writing*. Dallas, TX: Voyager Sopris Learning.

Classroom Scenario

Students in Mrs. Allen's sixth-grade class begin a unit of study with a discussion of how they can demonstrate their understandings at the end of the unit. The standards to be assessed are identified for the students and they brainstorm possible methods to assess their understandings. Mrs. Allen serves in a facilitative role during this process and is careful not to provide too much support. Once students have generated four or five viable products, they select the group they will work with based on the product they would like to use to demonstrate their learning. This interest-based grouping method works well for Mrs. Allen's students, giving them the freedom to connect with other learners seeking the same outcomes.

Complexity of Thinking Skills

Memorization or repetition required. Memorization is a simple task that requires repetition for many students.

Comprehension and understanding required. Students must be able to demonstrate a basic understanding of the content to complete the task.

Application and analysis are required. Performance-based tasks that require the learner to analyze and apply the content in new ways increase the challenge.

Synthesis, evaluation, and creativity required. When students are functioning at the top levels of Bloom's taxonomy, the complexity of the thinking is at its highest. Rigor is derived from critical and creative thinking when students are engaged in complex thinking processes.

The Continuum of Complexity is a tool that can be used with learners at any level. Adjusting complexity offers you the ability to keep students working with the same content while maintaining an engaging and purposeful learning environment without the difficulty of creating multiple lesson structures. Achieving the highest levels of complexity for all is not the goal; rather, the goal is to increase the complexity to support learners by keeping their brains engaged. Incremental increases in complexity can have a significant impact on the learning process. Raising the complexity in a single realm can keep a learner in productive struggle, a necessary ingredient for success. If a student demonstrates that he or she is moving into destructive struggle, the level of complexity may have been raised too quickly or in too many areas. Complexity ignites the brain and the learning process!

Strategy 2: Develop Depth of Knowledge

Dr. Norman Webb's depth of knowledge (DOK) model offers a clear and concise way to design content-based learning tasks that challenge students and place them in productive struggle, which increases their complexity of thinking and establishes a rigorous learning environment. Educators seeking to enhance the thinking within their classrooms can support the process by developing DOK "Level 3: Strategic Thinking" and "Level 4: Extended Thinking" activities (see **figure 5.2**). These tasks require the learner to engage in complex learning situations. The DOK structure can expand student understanding within a unit of study or as a follow-up to a unit of study. Through the development of these extension lessons, you can address the varied learning modalities of your students.

Figure 5.2 Webb's Depth of Knowledge: Context Ceilings[4]

DOK Level 1

Recall & Reproduction

Who?
What?
Where?
When?

DOK Level 2

Basic Application of Skills & Concepts

How did it happen?
Why did it happen?
How does it work?
Why does it work that way?

DOK Level 3

Strategic Thinking

How can you use it?
Why can you use it?
What is the cause?
What is the effect?
What is the reason?
What is the result?

DOK Level 4

Extended Thinking

What is the impact?
What is the influence?
What is the relationship?
What if?
What would happen?
What could happen?
What do you think, feel, believe?

DOK LEVELS OF COGNITIVE RIGOR

The depth of knowledge model categorizes tasks according to the cognitive rigor and complexity of thinking required to successfully complete them. The questions in each section offer possible task focus points for the teacher to use in the development of activities at each of the DOK levels. It is important to remember that the focus is on the complexity of the task that follows the verb rather than the verb used to describe the activity. These questions are designed to support the teacher and the learner in the development of tasks structured for different levels of complexity.

DOK Level 1: Recall and Reproduction

Tasks at this level require recalling facts or rote application of simple procedures. The tasks do not require any cognitive effort beyond remembering the right response or formula. Copying, computing, defining, and recognizing are typical level 1 tasks.

DOK Level 2: Skills and Concepts

At this level, students must "do something" with the content; they must make some decisions about their approach. Level 2 tasks usually require more than one mental step such as comparing, organizing, summarizing, predicting, and estimating.

DOK Level 3: Strategic Thinking

At this level of complexity, students use at least three resources. Students must use planning and evidence, and thinking is more abstract. Level 3 tasks involve multiple valid responses and students must justify their choices. Examples include solving

---

4. Adapted from work by Erik M. Francis, Maverik Education (maverikeducation.com), copyright © 2014.

nonroutine problems, designing an experiment, or analyzing characteristics of a genre. You may notice that the words *design* and *analyze* are also frequently used when developing level 4 tasks. Designing an experiment requires level 3 strategic thinking; however, if the student were to design, conduct, *and* analyze the experimental outcomes, they would then be functioning at the highest level of complexity, level 4.

DOK Level 4: Extended Thinking

Level 4 tasks require the most complex cognitive effort and use at least four resources. Students synthesize information from multiple sources, often over an extended period of time, or transfer knowledge from one or two domains to solve problems in another. Designing a survey and interpreting the results, analyzing multiple texts to extract themes, or writing an original myth in an ancient style are all examples of level 4.

The following example uses the verb "describe" differently in each activity. In this structure, what follows the verb determines the level of complexity of the activity. The level of complexity is vastly different in each activity.

Describe three characteristics of metamorphic rock. (Recall task: DOK Level 1)

Describe the differences between metamorphic and igneous rock. (Requires determination of differences between rock types: DOK Level 2)

Describe a model that you might use to represent the relationships that exist within the rock cycle. (Requires strategic understanding of the rock cycle and a determination of how to best represent it: DOK Level 3)

When lesson planning, remember that DOK levels are not sequential nor are they developmental. Giving students tasks at levels 3 and 4 can provide the context and motivation needed to engage learners better than tasks at the more routine learning levels 1 and 2. Even the youngest learners are capable of strategic and extended thinking. All students need the opportunity to engage in complex thinking.

As a teacher, you are likely often locked into instructing at levels 1 and 2. The tasks you present to students are geared to these two levels. However, generalizable learning occurs when students are working in Level 3: Strategic Thinking. "Teach in 3" is a concept that encourages teachers to instruct learners at the strategic thinking level. This requires students to do more than just use the content; they must justify their choices and determine the most viable solution. As learners, they remember what they need to know; teaching at the strategic level provides that "need to know" learning opportunity. When students are instructed at DOK Level 3, the instructional methods and activities can be scaffolded using varied levels of complexity to adjust for student readiness. Student engagement increases when learners participate in seeking the information needed.

Figure 5.3 gives sample activities for the four DOK levels. A template for extension lessons based on DOK is available on page 139.

	Figure 5.3 Sample Activities at All DOK Levels
DOK Level 1	Given a diagram of the heart, *label* the parts listed and show the flow of blood. *Sequence* the directions for making the paper airplane from the story.
DOK Level 2	A client is looking for a rectangular ottoman. He wants one with the most storage space possible but needs a height between 14 and 16 inches. What are the options available in a rectangular design? Identify the *cause/effect* relationships in the short story.
DOK Level 3	*Evaluate* how the different backgrounds and cultures of the characters in the story impacted the events and outcome of the story. *Develop* a model to represent the relationship between lift and drag.
DOK Level 4	*Connect* two of the common themes discussed in class across texts in different cultures. *Create* representations of the three data sources that would lead the audience to come to different conclusions regarding the data.

Strategy 3: Grouping and Personalized Learning: A Perfect Match

Differentiation is not about creating an individualized program for every student. It's about creating a personalized learning environment. Personalized learning is everywhere in our ever-changing world of education. The potential in personalized learning is immense; educators see it as a way to address the learning needs of a student population that grows more diverse by the day. In this section, we will look at the definition and the impact of personalized learning on students, particularly in groups, in today's technology-infused classrooms.

The idea of personalizing learning is not new. Teachers have long worked to design and implement instruction to address the varied learning needs of their students. However, the advent of technology in the classroom allows the student to take more ownership of the learning environment. Technology has opened the door to learning experiences never before available that can be tailored to students' learning needs. Likewise, the collection of data through digital resources enables teachers to focus closely on individual student performances. However, teachers and districts struggle with balancing the protection of private student data with the collection of information designed to develop and implement personalized learning. The challenge lies in bringing all the elements together to generate new and vibrant learning opportunities for students.

While the rise of personalized learning may be connected to technology, it does much more than, for example, adjust text reading levels using an application. Its goal is to provide a combination of learning activities that are aligned to a student's needs, thus offering a personalized learning experience. The focus lies with the student, not with the curriculum or the teacher, taking into account the student's strengths, weaknesses, personal interests, and motivation. Conceptually, personalized learning requires a deep commitment to the learning process, similar to project-based learning (PBL) and working with DOK levels.

DEFINITIONS AND CORE BELIEFS OF PERSONALIZED LEARNING

In 2010, three organizations—the Software & Information Industry Association, a Washington-based trade organization; ASCD, a nonprofit focused on curriculum development; and the Council of Chief State School Officers—participated in a symposium that produced the "Essential Elements and Policy Enablers for Personalized Learning," described in **figure 5.4**. The "Essential Elements" were items the team felt were fundamental to personalized learning. "Policy Enablers" were the steps administration needed to follow to allow the full use of the personalized learning format. The group emphasized the value of project-based learning and an increase in student ownership of learning goals. Technology and equity in access were believed to play a vital role in the development of personalized learning.

Figure 5.4 Essential Elements and Policy Enablers for Personalized Learning	
ESSENTIAL ELEMENTS	**POLICY ENABLERS**
1. Flexible, Anytime, Everywhere Learning	1. Redefine Use of Time
2. Redefine Teacher Role and Expand "Teacher"	2. Performance-Based, Time-Flexible Assessment
3. Project-Based, Authentic Learning	3. Equity in Access to Technology Infrastructure
4. Student-Driven Learning Path	4. Funding Models That Incentivize Completion
5. Mastery/Competency-Based Progression/Pace	5. P-20 Continuum and Non-Age/Grade Band System

In 2014, organizations including the Bill & Melinda Gates Foundation, the Michael & Susan Dell Foundation, and EDUCAUSE sought to create a working definition for personalized learning. Their definition has four basic tenets (see **figure 5.5**).

■ Students should follow a "competency-based progression" through topics.

■ Learning environments should be flexible and structured in a way to support students' goals.

■ Students should have personal learning paths.

■ Each student should have a learner profile.

Figure 5.5 Personalized Learning: A Working Definition[5]

A group of philanthropies and school and technology advocacy groups, with contributions from educators, compiled a four-part "working definition" of the attributes of personalized learning. They also identified critical questions for K–12 officials to consider in implementing personalized learning.

COMPETENCY-BASED PROGRESSION	FLEXIBLE LEARNING ENVIRONMENTS	PERSONAL LEARNING PATHS	LEARNER PROFILES
Each student's progress toward clearly defined goals is continually assessed. A student advances and earns credit as soon as he/she demonstrates mastery.	Student needs drive the design of the learning environment. All operational elements—staffing plans, space utilization, and time allocation—respond and adapt to support students in achieving their goals.	All students are held to clear, high expectations, but each student follows a customized path that responds and adapts based on his/her individual learning progress, motivations, and goals.	Each student has an up-to-date record of his/her individual strengths, needs, motivations, and goals.

Ongoing Assessment
In what ways and how frequently should we assess each student's level of mastery within the dimensions that we believe are essential for his/her success?

Individual Advancement
Can individual students pursue new learning experiences as soon as they have mastered the prerequisite content? How can students attain course credit based on mastery?

Operational Alignment
How might we deliver all the learning experiences that our students need, with the resources we have available? What flexibility is in the design to enable us to respond and adapt to changing student needs?

Staffing & Roles
In what ways might we structure teacher and other educator roles to support our instructional vision? What flexibility is needed to enable our staff to respond and adapt to changing student needs?

Time Allocation
In what ways might we maximize the time each student spends pursuing his/her goals? How might our student and staff schedules respond and adapt to changing student needs?

Space Utilization
How can the design of the physical space support our instructional vision? Can we use spaces beyond our walls, and if so, how?

Grouping & Connections
How should we group students to enable the varied learning experiences we hope to offer and modify to their changing needs? In what ways might we facilitate personal connections among students, and between students and adults?

Personalized Learning Plans
How can we ensure that each student has a learning plan that takes into account his/her strengths, changing needs, motivations, and goals?

Varied Learning Experiences (Modalities)
What types of experiences (for example, complex tasks, experiential learning) do students need to achieve their goals? What are the ideal methods for delivering (for example, small-group instruction, one-on-one tutoring, online learning) these experiences?

Student Ownership
In what ways might we enable students to develop and manage their own learning paths?

Strengths & Needs
How do we capture each student's current level of mastery within each of the dimensions that we believe are essential for his/her success (for example, academic standards, skills)? How can we highlight students' academic gaps to draw attention to their individual needs?

Motivations
How might we support each student in understanding and articulating his/her interests and aspirations?

Information & Feedback
In what ways and how frequently might we provide timely, actionable information and feedback to students, teachers, and families?

Goals
How might we support each student in setting personalized goals within each dimension that we believe is essential for his/her success? In what ways and how frequently might we ask students to reflect on their progress and adjust their goals accordingly?

5. Developed by the Bill & Melinda Gates Foundation, Afton Partners, the Eli & Edythe Broad Foundation, CEE Trust, the Christensen Institute, Charter School Growth Fund, EDUCAUSE, iNACOL, the Learning Accelerator, the Michael & Susan Dell Foundation, Silicon Schools, and educators across the United States. Funding provided by the Bill & Melinda Gates Foundation. www.edweek.org/ew/collections/personalized-learning-special-report-2014/a-working-definition.html. This graphic originally appeared in *Education Week* (October 22, 2014). Reprinted with permission from Editorial Projects in Education.

Personalized learning requires that we rethink and reorganize what we view as the "school" system. Teachers become coaches and facilitators rather than the sources of knowledge. Students can form personalized learning teams, learning independently and in collaborative groups. This learning environment does not seek to replace the teacher but rather to redefine the teacher's role. In a personalized learning classroom, the relationship between teacher and learner is essential, and it relies on the ability of the teacher to know his or her learners.

Barbara Bray and Kathleen McClaskey share the following core beliefs (see **figure 5.6**) regarding personalized learning in their book *Make Learning Personal.*

Figure 5.6 Twelve Core Beliefs of Personalized Learning[6]
1. Successful learners understand how they learn best.
2. An abundance of resources is available now to make learning personal.
3. Universal Design for Learning (UDL) is the framework to make learning personal for *all* learners.
4. Technology levels the playing field by removing barriers to learning.
5. Learners learn best in a creative, flexible environment.
6. Learners have a choice in how they acquire information and knowledge.
7. Learners have a voice in how they express what they know and understand.
8. Learners who own their learning are intrinsically motivated to learn and succeed.
9. The community can be the school. Everyone is a learner and a teacher.
10. Learning is a process and failure is a learning opportunity.
11. Everything can be a teachable moment.
12. Making learning personal is a cost-effective way to teach and learn.

Personalized learning offers unique opportunities for today's students. Placing ownership in the hands of the learner creates an environment that is rich, diverse, and ever-changing as learners grow and evolve. Allowing learners to build their own learning communities effectively generates groupings based on student interests, abilities, and skills.[7]

Strategy 4: Grouping for Multiple Intelligences

Howard Gardner's theory of multiple intelligences (MI) emerged from cognitive research and proposes that students have different kinds of minds and therefore learn, remember, perform, and understand in different ways. According to MI theory, each learner has preferred learning styles that help him or her maximize the learning process. Individuals differ in the strength of these intelligences and in the ways the

---

6. Adapted from Bray, B., and McClaskey, K. (2015). *Make Learning Personal: The What, Who, WOW, Where, and Why.* Thousand Oaks, CA: Corwin Press. Used with permission.
7. Bray, B., and McClaskey, K. (2015).

intelligences combine to help learners carry out different tasks and solve problems. When grouping using an MI structure, consider varied formats, such as grouping the visual/spatial learners in a group or placing your linguistic learners together. Another option is to provide each group with students of varied learning styles, thus allowing them to work together to showcase their strengths.

The MI Learning Styles Chart (**figure 5.7**) describes each intelligence included in MI theory and conventional ways each style can be taught in the classroom.

Figure 5.7 The MI Learning Styles Chart

LEARNING STYLE	DESCRIPTION OF LEARNERS	WAYS LEARNING STYLE IS TAUGHT
Visual-Spatial	Are aware of environments, see relationships and patterns in the world around them	Drawings, verbal and visual imagery, charts, graphics, photographs
Bodily-Kinesthetic	Have a keen sense of body awareness, use body effectively	Physical activity, hands-on learning, role-playing
Musical	Are sensitive to rhythms and sounds	Music or rhythm, multimedia
Interpersonal	Have social understanding and strong interaction skills	Group activities, dialogues, audio/video conferencing
Intrapersonal	Have strong understanding of own goals, may appear shy and struggle with group tasks	Independent study
Verbal-Linguistic	Possess highly developed auditory skills, think in words	Word games, reading, say-and-see concepts
Logical-Mathematical	Think conceptually and abstractly, can see and explore patterns and relationships	Experiments, logic activities, investigations, concepts prior to dealing with details
Naturalist	Ability to identify and distinguish among different types of plants, animals, and weather formations found in the natural world	Experiments, classifying, exploring the environment, categorizing information for further exploration

The Planning Model for Multiple Intelligences (**figure 5.8**) by Dr. Nina Greenwald offers specific lesson planning ideas that support each of the different learning preferences. The wheel provides examples of tasks to draw from when designing learning activities with specific MI learning styles in mind. Consider allowing your students to self-select which group they will work with according to their preferred learning style. This presents another student-directed way to form flexible learning groups.

Figure 5.8 Planning Model for Multiple Intelligences[8]

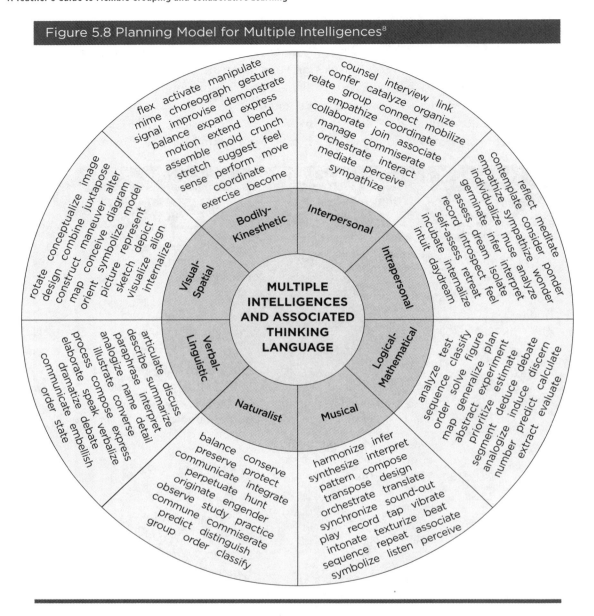

Strategy 5: Project-Based Learning

Project-based learning (PBL) is another instructional method through which students gain knowledge and skills by working for an extended time to investigate and respond to a complex question, problem, or challenge. This method of instruction encompasses multiple components of an authentic learning process:

- significant content
- 21st century competencies
- in-depth inquiry
- driving questions
- need to know

8. Greenwald, N. (November/December 1998). "Songs the Dinosaurs Sang." *Gifted Child Today*, 21(6). Image adapted and used with permission.

- student voice and choice
- critique and revision
- public audience

PBL is challenging, differentiated, rigorous, technology-infused, and focused on real-world issues. The emphasis is on the process rather than on a culminating project. For the purposes of this book, we focus on the grouping structures found within the PBL framework.

Grouping is an integral structure within the PBL environment. Without effective grouping, the collaborative energies needed for successful implementation can easily be missed. Efforts to purposefully group students can establish a learning environment that withstands various demands. Students remain in their learning groups anywhere from two to eight weeks. In setting up groups for the best possible success, make sure to consider all forces at work, such as behavior, ELL needs, academic ability, or artistic ability.

The PBL process requires collaborative work. Teamwork is a primary component in project-based learning, but that doesn't mean students automatically know how to work well together. Helping students make the most of team opportunities by deliberately teaching and modeling collaboration strategies supports the process. Social media applications like Edmodo, Google Hangouts, or other options allow students to interact on a digital platform. Using these applications, you can document students' collaboration, contributions, and engagement. Your students can use these applications to share ideas, and you can use them to formatively assess students' knowledge of the content.

Encourage collaboration within the groups by having students draw up a team contract that describes members' responsibilities. Students are more likely to follow norms when they create them as a group. Include reflection activities to encourage students to think about how well the teams are working or to raise red flags if they need help getting back on track.

Building dynamic groups that foster collaborative effort is well worth your while. Even in situations with purposeful grouping, however, conflicts will surface. Allow students to work through issues as they arise. When conflict arises within groups, be present but don't intervene unless necessary. Group collaboration teaches students how to solve conflicts. As shared in **figure 5.9**, there are multiple outcomes from PBL that significantly impact student learning.

Figure 5.9 Key Points in Developing Rigorous PBL	
KEY POINTS	**OUTCOMES**
Establish **real-world** connections.	Students are more engaged when learning relates directly to the world they live in.
Build a project that is core to the learning goals and **standards-based**.	Do not leave the standards behind. Challenge your students and align with core learning goals.
Structure **collaboration** for student success.	Provide a unique opportunity to help students practice critical thinking, collaboration, communication, and creativity.

continued →

Figure 5.9. Key Points in Developing Rigorous PBL, continued	
KEY POINTS	**OUTCOMES**
Facilitate the learning process in a **student-driven** learning environment.	When students are directly involved in planning and steering projects, they are more invested in their learning. Empower your students to work independently.
Embed **assessment** throughout the project.	Assessment can be integrated seamlessly into project-based learning. Measure student understanding from the beginning to the end of a project. Remember to assess the process, not just the product.

PBL projects can be simple or quite complex, as the following examples show. The Lemonade Stand (**figure 5.10**) is an example of using a simulation to introduce a PBL experience. Students are given the opportunity to play the simulation and then develop their own business. The use of the simulation helps learners with limited background experience the business world in a format where they can manipulate many variables. The Lemonade Stand is an example of a project that guides students through the process of business ownership.

Figure 5.10 PBL Example: Lemonade Stand[9]	
Description of purpose	Businesses are formed to sell products or services to make a profit for the person(s) owning the business. Businesses also provide valuable products or services that some members of the public need or want.
Product	If you were to start your own business, what sort of business would you create, and why? What are some things you could do to ensure success and avoid failures? How would your business compete against other similar businesses? Why would people buy your products or services over those of other businesses?
Content area	Social studies
Standards	Social Studies 4-1 ■ Identify the productive resources needed to produce a good or service and suggest opportunity costs for the resources involved. Social Studies 4-3 ■ Explain how entrepreneurs organize productive resources to produce goods and services and that they seek to make profits by taking risks.
Inspiration starting point	Play "Lemonade Tycoon," a simulation game available at someschoolgames.com/kids-games/lemonade-tycoon.
Estimated time	2–3 weeks
Suggested materials	Local phone book Internet access

---

9. Adapted from Stanley, T. (2012). *Project-Based Learning for Gifted Students: A Handbook for the 21st-Century Classroom.* Waco, TX: Prufrock Press, 116. Copyright 2012 by Prufrock Press. Used with permission.

When initiating a PBL project, start small. Focus on a few standards. The Lemonade Stand is a good example of setting a realistic goal. Concentrate the learning on one subject rather than multiple disciplines. PBL emphasizes in-depth inquiry, and quality not quantity. Make sure that the project won't take more than two to three weeks. You want to keep it focused and ensure authenticity and a public audience for your students. Instead of doing real-life fieldwork, consider having the learning occur in the classroom through a simulation format, like the one shown in Lemonade Stand. As students work through the simulation, they are immersed in the process of owning a business.

One of the challenges of PBL is the planning process. In PBL, you plan upfront. By working in reverse, you can map out a project that's ready to go in the classroom. Once you plan it, you're free to differentiate instruction and meet the immediate needs of your students (rather than being in panic mode trying to figure out what will happen tomorrow!). Mapping out the project day by day is an easy way to plan the process. With PBL, the project itself is the learning, not the "dessert" at the end. You teach throughout the project. The Buck Institute for Education's "Essential Project Design Elements Checklist" on page 140 is a great way to make sure you are focusing on critical aspects of the model, such as inquiry, voice and choice, and significant content.

Figure 5.11 is an example of a more complex fourth-grade project called Preserving the Past. It is designed to take place over a longer period than the Lemonade Stand. Multiple standards are addressed throughout the project process.

Figure 5.11 PBL Example: Preserving the Past[10]

Project Idea: Students invent a way to preserve a piece of a town's old train depot.
Entry Event: The town of Rainelle needs to remove one of its original landmarks, the train depot. The town's historical society has hired a group of students to come up with an idea for how to preserve a small piece of the train depot. The final project will be presented to the Rainelle Town Council at City Hall during the council's monthly meeting.

OBJECTIVES DIRECTLY TAUGHT OR LEARNED THROUGH DISCOVERY	IDENTIFIED LEARNING TARGETS	EVIDENCE OF SUCCESS IN ACHIEVING IDENTIFIED LEARNING TARGET
M.O.4.3.3	Students will measure length, create angles, mark and fit together the wood to make the final product.	Final product will be used to conclude if the student has achieved the learning target.
M.O.4.4.3	Students use tape measure and carpenter's square to measure.	Student observation, discussion, and collaboration during process will be observed and monitored to make sure the students stay focused on their learning target.

continued →

10. Adapted from "Teach 21: Preserving the Past." West Virginia Education Information System. Used with permission.

Figure 5.11 PBL Example: Preserving the Past,[10] continued

OBJECTIVES DIRECTLY TAUGHT OR LEARNED THROUGH DISCOVERY	IDENTIFIED LEARNING TARGETS	EVIDENCE OF SUCCESS IN ACHIEVING IDENTIFIED LEARNING TARGET
RLA.O.4.1.14	Students visit various websites to gather information about the town and background information on the train depot. While conducting interviews, students will take notes, paraphrase, summarize, question, and record data.	Teacher will meet and observe small groups to monitor their success in researching. Levels of monitoring will be determined by students' need for instruction with research. Students reflect on the process and progress of their research using journal entries. Students record which resources contained valuable information and which did not.
RLA.O.4.1.15	Students develop diagrams, flowcharts, or layout of ideas for the final project. Use computer program (e.g., Inspiration or Popplet) to create a visual web.	Group will present their final diagram to the class.
RLA.O.4.2.12	Students will research using current local newspapers, news archives, and periodicals.	Students interview residents and family members associated with the town and depot. Audio or video recordings will be used to document.
SS.O.04.05.12	Students will collect and label memorabilia.	Information acquired will be presented by each student to the class.
SS.O.04.04.03	Students will understand the hardships of transportation in the 1920s to 1970s and the importance the railroad played in the economic and social development of the town.	Students interview residents and family members associated with the town and depot. They record written entries of interviews and any other media presented by the interviewee, e.g., pictures, trinkets, memorabilia.
SS.O.04.04.02	Students will understand the hardships of transportation in the 1920s to 1970s and the importance the railroad played in the economic and social development of the town.	Students interview residents and family members associated with the town and depot. They record written entries of interviews and any other media presented by the interviewee, e.g., pictures, trinkets, memorabilia.
VA.O.4.1.03	Students transfer a picture to watercolor format. Students use watercolor to create a painting.	Teacher observes the activity of the students creating their artwork. The artwork will be displayed at school. Students will take knowledge acquired from the activity and teach the preK class how to make a watercolor of their own pictures.

Strategy 6: Encourage Active Questioning

Questioning strategies are one of the best (and easiest) ways to differentiate instruction. Today's learners must be able to understand the questioning process and use it to their advantage. Gone are the days when it was sufficient to simply teach students the answers to questions. Students must now learn how to generate the questions.

The learners in our classrooms must know how to ask the right kinds of questions so they can seek answers for problems that have not yet developed. Ask yourself: Am I teaching my students to question or am I simply providing answers? Textbooks provide answers; they allow a student to move into the passive absorption of information. Textbooks are valuable but only as a resource or tool; they should not supplant the inquiry process.

You no doubt ask your students numerous questions each day. Be careful that these questions do not fall into the realm of passive questioning. Passive questions are those asked *of* a student. They may have multiple responses, but the process fosters compliance rather than engagement on the part of the learner. Instead, your job is to engage students in active questioning. Active questions are those asked *by* the student that demonstrate the student's understanding and desire to delve more deeply into the content. Active questions engage the learner in the process of learning.

Classroom Scenario

Teams of four and five students are scattered about the classroom researching a topic Mr. Naylor has just introduced. Some teams are pouring over books piled high on tables, while others search internet sites on various tech devices. Large chart papers line the board. Each chart contains a broad, essential question and is covered with dozens of colored sticky notes.

The groups have been brainstorming questions related to the topic of exploration as they conduct their research. They write their questions on the sticky notes and place them on the chart paper under the appropriate essential question posted by Mr. Naylor. The room buzzes with energy! These students are not looking for answers; they are learning to seek the questions that will drive their study of the topics they will be investigating.

Meaningful questions can teach students many things. Questions encourage students to use their imaginations, to listen to others and their ideas, and to engage in new ways of thinking about familiar things. The expression and sharing of ideas is accomplished at the highest levels through active questioning.

Figure 5.12 The Do's and Don'ts of Questioning	
DO . . .	**DON'T . . .**
ask open-ended questions.	ask questions to find out what learners don't know.
accept all answers.	ask questions that have a right or wrong answer.
use Think Pair Share to foster discussion.	allow students to make fun of a creative or unusual response.

continued →

Figure 5.12 The Do's and Don'ts of Questioning, continued

DO . . .	DON'T . . .
reward the responding, not the response.	ask questions in isolation of content.
ask questions that stir emotions.	stick to the questions in the teacher's edition of textbook.
allow wait time; not everyone processes at the same speed.	let students "pass" when asked a question. (Use question buddies to avoid this.)
ask questions that have no definitive answer.	use raised hands to identify the student who will respond to the question.
listen to each response.	allow students to give up! Learning to be a good questioner takes time and lots of practice.
create a system for asking and answering questions.	underestimate your students' imaginations.

WHY QUESTION? IT'S SIMPLE!

Questions can stretch the thinking of your students. With passive questioning, once an answer is given, the thinking process stops. Keeping the thinking and learning process active allows for more divergent and high-level student responses.

Active questions:

- Improve listening
- Increase engagement
- Develop metacognitive skills
- Further imagination
- Stretch students' thinking

Good questions lead us to ask more questions while the learning process continues.

Classroom Scenario

Ms. Lanoi posts the question, "Are we prejudiced in today's society?" on the whiteboard as her sixth graders enter the room. The class has been investigating the concept of prejudice from a historical perspective. It's time to bring the topic closer to home. She asks them, "What do you need to know before you answer that question? What are your own questions?" Students begin generating questions to further their research. The questions are posted on chart paper around the room. Students self-select their groups based on the question they want to research. The questions lead to more questions, and the next step for these learners is to refine their topics even further by identifying additional questions to which they need answers. Ms. Lanoi moves from group to group, noting the level of questions the students are generating. She is quick to note those learners that may require additional scaffolding in the process of building their questions. Two of her special education students and her ELL learners are struggling with how to build their questions. She has a questioning template ready to support these learners, which allows the learning flow to continue and the students to remain a part of the learning experience. The groups are working at a high level of complexity in their question design. By starting with a Beyond the Line question (see **figure 5.13**), students learn that they will need to make a judgment and then pull from multiple sources to support their decision.

QUESTIONING TYPES AND EXAMPLES

In this section, we describe nine types of questioning and provide examples of their use for the different levels of learning groups. Figure 5.13 provides an overview of these question types.

Figure 5.13 Nine Question Types

TYPE	BRIEF DESCRIPTION	EXAMPLES
On the Line	Literal; answer is within the text	What was the name of Tyler's dog?
Between the Lines	Requires inference using information provided	Why was the dog so important to Tyler?
Beyond the Line	Requires judgment and additional information	Why does Tyler feel he needs a therapy dog? Do you agree or disagree?
Document-Based Questions (DBQ)	Can be answered with the textual evidence provided Support analysis of text	The Great Wall helped isolate China from Europe and the Middle East. Was this a good idea? Why? As a banned person, what restrictions does Nelson Mandela face?
De Bono's Thinking Hats ■ Green ■ White ■ Yellow ■ Black ■ Blue ■ Red	Guide learners in looking at the content through various lenses, allowing them to see the information from multiple perspectives	*Green*: What ideas are possible? *White*: What information do I need? *Yellow*: What's the advantage of this idea? *Black*: What are the possible hazards involved? *Blue*: What are the next steps? *Red*: What is my intuition telling me about this situation?
Divergent Questions	Seek multiple answers Are open-ended	How might life in the year 2100 differ from today? If computers correct spelling, is it necessary for third graders to take spelling tests?
Preference Questions	Require learners to make a decision; to choose	Would you rather eat a piece of cake or a cupcake? Would you rather ride in a car, on a train, or in a plane?

continued →

Figure 5.13 Nine Question Types, continued

TYPE	BRIEF DESCRIPTION	EXAMPLES
Personification Questions	Offer insight into a student's true depth of understanding Encourage personal connections	What would a tear say to a smile? What would an igneous rock say to a volcano?
What If? Questions	Unlock the imagination Stretch the thought process	What if water wasn't wet? What if time really did stand still?
Costa's Three Levels of Questioning ■ Gathering ■ Processing ■ Applying	Tools to support students in the process of question development	*Gathering*: What formula would you use in this situation? *Processing*: What is the message in this event? *Applying*: What significance is this event in the global perspective?
Justification Questions	Seek to prompt students to defend their thinking Students learn to question the validity of information and conclusions drawn	How might the conclusion drawn be supported with evidence from the text? What information is needed to provide validity to the claim?

On the Line/Between the Lines/Beyond the Line Questions

Understanding the types of questions supports students in the learning process. One way to think about questions relates to how the answer to the question will be achieved. In any given class, you may have students working at each of these levels of questioning.

On the Line questions are those literal questions often used to determine basic understanding of material. Teaching students to recognize this type of question directs them to seek the answer directly from the text. Students can learn to skim and scan text for these answers.

Between the Lines questions are more inferential. A simple skim and scan will not suffice. Students must read the text to make connections between information shared to identify the appropriate response.

Beyond the Line questions are more reflective. To respond to these questions, students must make connections within the text and with other ideas related to the text. These questions ask the learner to make evaluative judgments about the information they are reading. Often these questions require students to pull from multiple resources. Asking students to contemplate the bigger idea, a beyond the line question might ask, "Is violence ever justified?" or "Based on your research, defend or refute the following statement: We are destined to repeat the errors of the past; history is truly a repetitive process." This type of question pushes students beyond the text and engages them in complex thinking.

Document-Based Questions (DBQ)

Document-based questions give students practice working with primary and secondary source materials. These questions address a variety of common social studies and science topics and prepare students to do the work of historians and social scientists. DBQs provide students with opportunities to engage and wrestle with multiple pieces of documentary evidence.

Students construct essays, using several documents per paragraph to prove each part of their thesis. "Should recycling be required?" "Using the line graph, in what year was chlorine first added to the Philadelphia water supply?" "Based on the information in the text, did this curb typhoid fever?" Document-based questions help students understand the process of close analysis, interrogation of documents, and argument writing. Students learn to use textual evidence to respond to and support answers.

De Bono's Six Thinking Hats

De Bono's Six Thinking Hats, developed by thinking expert Edward de Bono, offer another key questioning technique. Each hat challenges the individual to view the information through a different lens (see **figure 5.14**). For example, the Green Hat asks the "wearer" to seek creative and innovative possibilities when viewing the information. The wearer is challenged to seek alternative solutions from the traditional approach and to encompass new ideas. The Black Hat asks the wearer to look through the lens of pessimism: "What possible difficulties will be encountered?" "What may impede the success of the endeavor?" The strategy supports the learner in seeing the information from all perspectives.

Figure 5.14 De Bono's Six Thinking Hats[11]		
Blue Hat	Process	Looks at the big picture. ▪ What thinking is needed? ▪ Where are we now? ▪ What do we need to do next?
Yellow Hat	Benefits	Sees the positives. ▪ Why is this a good idea? ▪ What are the advantages or benefits?
Green Hat	Creativity	Explores the creative aspects. ▪ What new ideas are possible? ▪ How might it be changed or improved?
Red Hat	Feelings	Deals with one's intuition or instinct. ▪ How do I feel about this? ▪ What's good about the way I feel, and what do I not like?
White Hat	Facts	Deals in only the facts. ▪ What do I know? ▪ What do I need to find out? ▪ How will I get the information that I need?
Black Hat	Caution	Looks at the negatives. ▪ What issues could arise? ▪ What are the disadvantages?

11. Adapted from the de Bono Group's "Six Thinking Hats." www.debonogroup.com/six_thinking_hats.php.

Divergent Questions

Divergent questioning strategies push students to seek multiple responses rather than a single answer. An easy way to understand this is by looking at reproductive versus productive questions. A reproductive question would be "What is 8 + 3?" The productive counterpart would be to ask the student, "How many ways can you make 11?" In language arts, a teacher might ask students to "List three important events in *Charlotte's Web*." The productive counterpart would be to ask the students to "Compare the events in *Charlotte's Web* with those from another text." In each instance the teacher is looking for multiple responses rather than a single answer. Questions that encourage and require students to compare information and ideas promote higher-level thinking strategies. Similes, metaphors, and analogies challenge students to make connections that they might not make on their own.

Preference Questions

Preference questions offer teachers insights into how students process and use information. These types of questions demand that a choice be made; there is no right or wrong answer. Some students struggle with the ambiguity of these types of questions, believing that there must be a right answer. The goal is to have the student make a choice and then support it. These types of questions can offer a way to connect with students in a nonthreatening way. A simple preference question might be, "Would you rather be a daisy or a dandelion, and why?" or "Would you rather be a video or a book, and why?" As students become more accustomed to these types of questions, they can be used to begin Socratic discussions, such as, "Would you rather lead or follow, and why?"

Personification Questions

Personification questions fall into a similar category as preference questions. Personification occurs when we personify an inanimate object; it is given human qualities and actions. These questions help students see a topic from a different perspective. "If yellow could talk, what would it say to red?" or "What would hope ask of despair?" Questions of this nature encourage students to think beyond the curriculum to make personal connections and define their understandings. Personification questions are rarely found in a textbook but offer us insights into the depth of student knowledge. Getting students out of their passive roles and into active participation is the goal of questioning. Letting your students create their own personification questions to use with the class can help them think critically and deepen discussion.

"What If?" Questions

"What If?" questions are some teachers' nightmare! The questions can be frustrating when students are unable to focus on the topic at hand. However, these types of questions do serve a valuable purpose. "What If?" questions are a reorganization of reality. They often hold the key to unlocking divergent thinking: laughter. You can start with a fun one: "What if humans walked on their hands instead of their feet?" And move to a thoughtful one: "What if Martin Luther King Jr. had been born in 1829 versus 1929?" These questions take thinking out of the box and can be used with any content area, topic, or grade level.

Costa's Three Levels of Questioning

Costa's Three Levels of Questioning, developed by education researcher Art Costa, provide yet another tool for question development. The Question House (see **figure 5.15**) is built with three stories:

Level 1: Gathering is the ground floor. This level provides the structure for the development of information-gathering questions. At this basic level of questioning, a student might be asked to "Identify five key events in the story."

Level 2: Processing is the second story. This level offers process questions. These questions require the individual to process the information and make an inference or draw a conclusion. At the second level, a student could be asked to "Tell me what is significant about the five key story events."

Level 3: Applying is the attic. This level supports the learner in developing questions of application. It is not enough to make an inference at this level; the student must apply the acquired knowledge to the situation. A third-level question might be, "What type of evidence is the most compelling to you?"

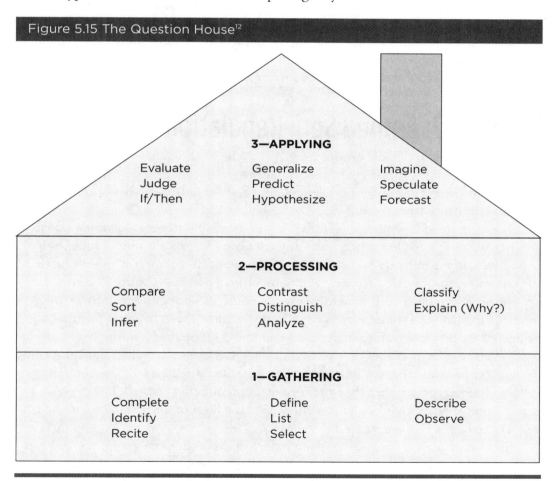

Figure 5.15 The Question House[12]

Learning how to seek information and recognizing what questions need to be asked is a vital skill for learners today. Both Costa's levels of questioning and Bloom's taxonomy focus on particular verbs to guide the level of questions developed. The

---

12. Adapted with permission from AVID Press of AVID Center, San Diego, California. www.avid.org.

key is to give students the tools to develop and ask meaningful questions that extend and expand their understandings. These structures help when teaching students how to develop questions. However, when designing learning activities, it is important to remember that the verb alone does not determine the rigor and complexity of the task; it is what follows the verb that determines its level of complexity, just as we discussed previously with DOK levels.

Justification Questions

With the advent of the Common Core State Standards, more and more students are required to justify their responses. Students must be able to provide evidence to support their reasoning. Teaching students how to recognize a justification question is the first step in their learning how to respond to it. As a learner, what one can identify, one can create. Students should learn how to answer a justification question and how to develop one. Justification questions help students critique the validity of information as well as the conclusions drawn from that information. These questions support students in becoming critical thinkers and questioners.

Questioning strategies represent the simplest form of differentiation yet potentially the most complex method for developing critical thinking. Teachers can vary and adjust questions to instantly challenge any student with no real advanced planning. Questioning methods become routine in highly effective teaching. The practice challenges advanced learners while encouraging all students to think critically.

Strategy 7: Embed Self-Regulation Skills

Students working in flexible groups must be able to work independently, manage their own learning tasks, set goals, assess their progress, manage their time, and recognize their own strengths and challenges. These self-regulation skills do not come naturally for many students; they need to be taught and modeled.

The level of independence you give to students is contingent on your students' ability levels and knowledge of a given topic. This means that, at times, students may be working independently on a project, and at other times, they may need a more structured process in place. Knowing how much independence your students need on a given task requires ongoing formative assessment. Strategies for short-term informal formative assessment are shared in this section. (See chapter 3 for methods of formal preassessments, formative assessments, and summative assessments.)

When working with lesson extensions, students develop self-direction, problem-solving, critical thinking, collaboration, and creativity. Attention to these skills impacts the *process* of learning rather than the specific content being learned. These are skills that, when well developed, enhance and elevate the level of understanding in whatever content area is being studied.

Encourage your students to use and reflect on these skills to strengthen and support desired learning behaviors. When embedding self-regulation skills into instruction, teachers typically begin emphasizing specific terminology related to the skills. This process helps all students derive a more thorough understanding of the content they are learning, particularly when engaged in extension activities in the higher DOK levels.

The five self-regulation skills described in the following sections assist students in learning how to manage their time and attention, set and complete goals, and monitor the efficacy of their efforts. These skills become crucial for students working on lesson extensions whether they are working independently, with a partner, or in a small group. The lists shown here provide specific objectives you can emphasize for this purpose.

SELF-DIRECTION

Educator Malcolm Knowles defines self-directed learning as follows: "In its broadest meaning, self-directed learning describes a process by which individuals take the initiative, with or without the assistance of others, in diagnosing their learning needs, formulating learning goals, identifying human and material resources for learning, choosing and implementing appropriate learning strategies, and evaluating learning outcomes."[13] The key point here is that learners take the initiative to pursue a specific learning experience and the responsibility for completing their learning. These skills can be explicitly taught.

You can emphasize the following objectives when teaching students to develop their abilities for self-direction:

- Set challenging, achievable goals and identify and access the resources necessary to achieve the goals.
- Manage time and resources in an efficient manner to achieve goals.
- Review progress and learning experiences to resolve problems that may be interfering with achieving goals.
- Ask others for feedback and seriously consider their ideas when revising work.
- Be determined to find an answer or solution to a problem and monitor one's commitment to goals using a variety of techniques to stay on task.
- Identify and describe the criteria and performance standards for quality work.
- Identify strengths and weaknesses of one's work in clear terms and identify areas for improvement.
- Reflect to set new goals and effectively incorporate information learned from successes and struggles.

These objectives allow students to create and keep to a schedule, monitor progress, and produce quality work. Engaging learners in productive struggle requires students to learn how to move forward even when their initial attempts have been unsuccessful. Teaching these structures helps students build independence and strengthen the ability to persevere.

PROBLEM-SOLVING

A major goal in education is to help students learn in ways that enable them to use their knowledge to solve problems in new situations. Problem-solving can be described as cognitive processing aimed at achieving a goal when no solution is obvious to the solver. Problem-solving is a process that involves reasoning, decision-making, and thinking critically. Many of the group extension activities in this book require that students use these problem-solving strategies.

---

13. Knowles, M. S. (1975). *Self-Directed Learning: A Guide for Learners and Teachers.* New York: Association Press, 18.

You can emphasize the following objectives when teaching students to build their abilities to problem solve:

- Carefully analyze all the characteristics of a problem before beginning to solve it.
- Identify important information needed to solve complex problems.
- Anticipate different kinds of problems in complex projects and think of ways to solve the problems before they happen.
- Use the strategies and tools learned along with subject-area knowledge to solve problems.
- Reflect on problem-solving efforts, evaluate the learning process, and make changes when necessary.

The ability to problem solve is critical for all students, whether working on teacher-structured tasks, working independently, or working in small groups on learning activities that are abstract and open-ended. Due to their open-ended nature, some lesson extension activities in the higher DOK levels require students to monitor their process and make adjustments when needed. Redirecting their efforts helps learners refine the quality of their work, further develop their ideas, and scrutinize the purpose of the activity.

CRITICAL THINKING

Critical thinking strategies play a dynamic role in every aspect of the learning process in an engaged classroom. Teachers seeking to differentiate curriculum for all learners and offer authentic learning experiences ensure that these strategies are interwoven into all the learning elements. Students engaged in the process of questioning and critiquing validity explore content through different lenses and construct an authentic foundation of understanding far beyond the recall level.

Critical thinking is an enhancement of the questioning process and is essential in every aspect of the curriculum. As discussed previously, thinking is not driven by answers but by questions. Extension activities provide questions that require students to think critically rather than simply answer a question. Richard Paul, director of research and professional development at the Center for Critical Thinking, defines critical thinking as, "thinking that analyzes thought, that assesses thought, and that transforms thought for the better . . . It's thinking about thinking while thinking in order to think better."[14] This process improves the ability to solve problems.

You can emphasize the following objectives when teaching students to build their abilities for critical thinking:

- Identify the most important parts of the information being studied.
- Use multiple strategies for evaluating the reliability of different kinds of sources.
- Use subject area knowledge and personal experiences to make connections and draw inferences between content areas.
- Clearly explain an opinion on a topic in speaking and in writing and give good reasons for it.

Given the independent nature of extension activities, students working in groups at appropriate DOK levels need the ability to think critically, which involves

---

14. Paul, R. (July 23, 2007). "Critical Thinking in Every Domain of Knowledge and Belief" keynote address. criticalthinking.org/pages/critical-thinking-in-every-domain-of-knowledge-and-belief/698.

analyzing information and supporting their methodology. They will often need to rely on previous learning experiences and consider prior knowledge when completing the learning activities. They will need to discern and evaluate relevancy when synthesizing material. And perhaps most importantly, critical thinking requires that students use analysis and criticism to determine the credibility of a source. The process requires both inductive and deductive reasoning skills. Inductive reasoning refers to the use of one's internal feelings about the information. It is tempered with factual evidence but relies on those gut emotions that guide our judgments. Deductive reasoning involves the process of considering all the facts and evidence available to make a decision based on the evidence. To be a strong critical thinker, both processes must come into play.

Much of the process relies on the ability to organize and validate the information presented. To this end, students must learn how to successfully manipulate graphic organizers as well as determine the credibility of the sources from which evidence is obtained. In **figure 5.16**, Richard Cash and Diane Heacox provide assessment questions to support critical thinking.

Figure 5.16 Assessment Questions for Critical Thinking[15]	
CRITICAL THINKING STRATEGY	**ASSESSMENT QUESTIONS**
Identifying main idea/argument	■ What is the main idea, point, or argument the author is making? ■ What specific points support the main idea, point, or argument? ■ How does the author resolve the argument?
Analyzing arguments	■ What evidence is used to support or contradict the argument? ■ What assumptions does the author rely upon? ■ What is the structure of the argument?
Compare and contrast	■ What are the specific elements of each item? ■ How can the elements be organized into categories of similarity and difference? ■ What are the principles that govern each of the elements?
Sequencing and prioritizing	■ In what way is the order or sequence important? ■ How might changing the order or sequence change the outcome? ■ Why is the order or sequence important?
Finding relevance and irrelevance	■ What information is relevant or irrelevant to the argument? ■ What makes the information relevant or irrelevant to the argument? ■ How can relevant/irrelevant information be made irrelevant/relevant?

continued →

15. Adapted from *Differentiation for Gifted Learners: Going Beyond the Basics*. Diane Heacox and Richard M. Cash (Minneapolis, MN: Free Spirit Publishing Inc., 2014). Used with permission.

	Figure 5.16 Assessment Questions for Critical Thinking,[15] continued
CRITICAL THINKING STRATEGY	**ASSESSMENT QUESTIONS**
Discerning fact vs. opinion	■ How can the facts be identified and validated? ■ How does the author use opinions to support or contradict the argument? ■ In what ways do the facts support or contradict opinions?
Investigating reliable and unreliable sources	■ What sources does the author use? ■ In what ways do the sources support or contradict the author's point? ■ How is a source validated or invalidated?
Distinguishing assumptions and generalizations	■ How does the author use assumptions in the argument? ■ What generalizations are made in the arguments? ■ How does the argument create assumptions or generalizations?
Identifying cause and effect	■ What are the specific causes and effects? ■ What would happen if a cause or effect were changed? ■ In what ways do the causes/effects predict the effects/causes?
Understanding point of view	■ How might the author's point of view develop? ■ How does the author's point of view affect the argument? ■ What is another point of view?
Recognizing bias and stereotype	■ What bias or stereotype is used to support or contradict the argument? ■ Why did the author use bias or stereotype in the argument?
Using deduction and induction	■ How does the author use a sequence to generate a conclusion? (Deductive) ■ How has the author used individual events to generate conclusions? (Inductive)

COLLABORATION

Flexible grouping allows learners to build upon their strengths while they learn the collaborative process. When students work collaboratively to solve problems, they share knowledge and develop skills that can lead to deeper learning and understanding. Collaborative learning has been shown to result in higher student achievement, higher self-esteem, and higher motivation for all students, across all socioeconomic and cultural backgrounds. Individual work can help a student master content, while group work empowers a student's resilience. When working collaboratively, students see each other as resources with whom they can test their own theories, determine if they are on the right track, and develop habits of mind. Keep in mind that students need guidance to learn to work together effectively.

You can emphasize the following objectives when teaching students to develop their abilities of collaboration:

- Actively contribute to the group by participating in discussions.
- Accept and perform all required tasks.
- Help the group set goals and direct the group in meeting them.
- Share ideas and contribute information appropriate for the topic.
- Encourage other members to share their ideas.
- Balance listening and speaking.
- Consider other people's feelings and ideas.
- Participate in the group assessment of how well members are working together.

Extension activities at all DOK levels can involve students working with partners or in small groups. However, some students may face challenges when working with peers. These students need to develop strategies for collaborating with others. They may also need to learn how to listen, how to take turns talking, and how to monitor oneself and others when working with peers.

CREATIVITY

To foster and nurture the growth of creativity, Dr. Paul Torrance advises teachers to encourage curiosity, exploration, experimentation, fantasy, questioning, testing, and the development of creativity. These processes should be inherent in all aspects of learning and in all subject areas.

You can emphasize the following objectives when helping students develop creativity:

- Use knowledge and skills in the subject matter to generate possible ideas.
- Seek out new experiences without worrying about making mistakes or what others think.
- Have confidence in one's ability to determine if ideas are worth pursuing.
- Add the necessary concrete details to an idea to make it a successful product or performance.
- Use language in meaningful and novel ways to move, inspire, entertain, inform, and persuade others.

Creativity abounds in students of all ages, especially in the youngest learners. However, allowing unlimited creativity has the potential to deter students from their learning goals. Lesson extensions are only valid when they further students' understanding of the content being considered. When students stray too far from the learning objectives, the lesson can become more of an unrelated enrichment activity rather than an extension of the objective.

All students can be creative while mastering learning objectives in all our students. Students working on activities at the higher DOK levels especially need to develop these skills. Encouraging a self-reflective process with your students not only enhances learning but helps prepare them for lifelong learning.

In Closing

This chapter discussed seven classroom strategies that extend group learning broadly and deeply in all content areas and at all learning levels. We discussed the critical role everyday methods like questioning strategies and increasing complexity can play in a classroom where students are working in groups at varying levels. We examined methods teachers can use to facilitate learning so that all students can think critically and embrace rigor. Finally, we discussed the importance of developing self-reflective skills that encourage critical and creative thinking while collaborating with peers in learning groups.

DOK Extension Lesson Template

Topic:

Content Standards:

Learning Activities

DOK Level 1:

DOK Level 2:

DOK Level 3:

DOK Level 4:

Essential Project Design Elements Checklist[*]

DOES THE PROJECT MEET THESE CRITERIA?	YES	NO	?
KEY KNOWLEDGE, UNDERSTANDING, AND SUCCESS SKILLS The project is focused on teaching students key knowledge and understanding derived from standards and success skills including critical thinking, problem-solving, collaboration, and self-management.			
CHALLENGING PROBLEM OR QUESTION The project is based on a meaningful problem to solve or a question to answer, at the appropriate level of challenge for students, which is operationalized by an open-ended, engaging driving question.			
SUSTAINED INQUIRY The project involves an active, in-depth process over time, in which students generate questions, find and use resources, ask further questions, and develop their own answers.			
AUTHENTICITY The project has a real-world context; uses real-world processes, tools, and quality standards; makes a real impact; and is connected to students' own concerns, interests, and identities.			
STUDENT VOICE & CHOICE The project allows students to make some choices about the products they create, how they work, and how they use their time, guided by the teacher and depending on their age and PBL experience.			
REFLECTION The project provides opportunities for students to reflect on what and how they are learning, and on the project's design and implementation.			
CRITIQUE & REVISION The project includes processes for students to give and receive feedback on their work to revise their ideas and products or to conduct further inquiry.			
PUBLIC PRODUCT The project requires students to demonstrate what they learn by creating a product that is presented or offered to people beyond the classroom.			

[*]Buck Institute for Education, bie.org, copyright © 2015. Used with permission.

CHAPTER 6
Differentiating Daily with Flexible Groups

GUIDING QUESTIONS
- What are some ways I can differentiate daily for all students?
- What does it mean to compact curriculum and why is it important when differentiating with groups?
- What are some instructional strategies to use with learning groups?

In this chapter, we describe instructional strategies that all teachers can use to differentiate curriculum throughout the school day. These strategies can be incorporated into various subject areas, take little preparation time, and are easy to incorporate into daily instruction and grouping practices. Although easily implemented, they provide depth and complexity as they appeal to students' varying interests and learning styles and help students at all levels engage in critical thinking.

In chapter 3 we discussed how to use assessments to form flexible learning groups. By using diagnostic and formative assessments throughout the learning process, you can determine how students are progressing and how to further differentiate activities and instruction for them based on their needs. When you create and differentiate instruction in groups based on solid assessment data, you are no longer making assumptions about what students know and don't know. Instead, you are grouping students together for a targeted purpose and teaching them the specific material they need and want to learn.

One key differentiation strategy we discuss is curriculum compacting, which is described in the following section. Many of the differentiation strategies shared in this chapter can be effectively used with students who have compacted out of the given material and require alternate learning activities. Understanding the purpose of curriculum compacting is foundational to using the strategies described in this chapter.

What Is Curriculum Compacting?

Compacting curriculum moves students out of curriculum they have already mastered and into new and challenging curriculum, so they can extend their learning. This method can occur one lesson at a time, one week at time, or an entire unit at a time. Documentation of mastery is an essential part of the curriculum compacting process. This option ensures that students are involved in a continuous learning process.

With curriculum compacting, it becomes necessary to develop alternative activities for students who have compacted out. These extension activities must be purposeful and meaningful to deepen thought and enrich learning. The activities may address student readiness, interests, and/or learning preferences, as well as specific content and curricular goals. Some extensions are designed purely as exploration endeavors. They are commonly interest-based activities that offer students the opportunity to delve deeply into a topic. Other extensions are more standards-driven and designed to provide students application opportunities for components of the unit of study. See the following scenarios for examples of compacting options.

Classroom Scenario

Mr. Franks enjoys using the "Most Difficult First" assessment strategy with his seventh-grade math class (see page 71 in chapter 3 for more on this strategy). This strategy allows him to provide single-lesson compacting. Mr. Franks teaches his five- to ten-minute lesson offering one or two examples. Students are then given the opportunity to complete the five most difficult problems. If the problems are completed accurately, the students are released from completing the remainder of the assignment and, instead, work on extension lessons. Students move into extension activities created by Mr. Franks to delve more deeply into the content being studied.

Students who are unable to accurately complete the challenging problems or have chosen not to attempt them will continue the lesson with Mr. Franks and complete the assigned guided practice and/or homework. This strategy enables Mr. Franks to move students out of curriculum they have already mastered.

Another compacting option is to give students the opportunity to pretest out of material prior to instruction. In this scenario, a pretest can be given covering a weekly unit such as spelling or vocabulary. For example, you give students a pretest of the material on Monday, and those students scoring 90 percent or higher compact out of the weekly activities associated with the content. These students continue their learning growth by engaging in extension activities, which are generally more complex activities that cover the same content. Following is another pretest compacting example.

Classroom Scenario

The fifth graders in Ms. Miller's class are preparing to begin their study of the Revolutionary War. Students are given a pretest covering the material to be studied. This diagnostic assessment provides Ms. Miller with valuable information about her learners. She quickly identifies seven students with extensive knowledge of the topic. Ms. Miller gives these students an opportunity to study a different revolutionary war and provides them three other revolutionary wars from which to select. The students explore how the war they select paralleled the American Revolution. To guide students, Ms. Miller provides a chart identifying the areas she would like them to focus on and a few specific criteria to include in their culminating project. They develop the learning plan and timeline together with specific checkpoints along the way. These students present their projects to all the fifth-grade classes when the unit is completed.

Strategies for Differentiating Daily for All Students

The differentiation strategies described in the following sections apply to all students: those who have compacted out of curriculum and those who require more scaffolding or practice. The strategies include: tiered lessons, thinking triangles, "I Am's," choice boards/extension menus, "make 10" boards, and restaurant menus. Although these strategies have been around for many years, we now encourage you to use them in conjunction with your grouping practices. Students are diverse in their learning needs. Flexible grouping, paired with daily differentiated instruction, helps you address the diversity of your students while maintaining a manageable environment for your classroom.

TIERED LESSONS

Tiered assignments blend assessment with instruction. Use pretest results to determine in which tier the students will be working. In this way, tiered lessons offer an opportunity to challenge each student at an appropriate level while keeping students in the same content. This format provides enrichment of the content, as well as acceleration through the process by adding complexity to the tasks. The Continuum of Complexity and DOK Levels (see chapter 5) are great tools for the development of a tiered lesson. Tiered lessons offer the learner different entry points into the content being addressed. See a reproducible planning chart for tiered lessons on page 153.

The objective in tiered instruction is to ensure that:

- All students are appropriately challenged.
- All learners invest approximately the same amount of time in the learning process.
- Every learner is learning something new.
- Every learner has the right to an equal amount of fun.

When creating tiered lessons, always start with the standard. The standard is the one component that cannot be differentiated. Once you have determined the standard, you are ready to build the tiered lesson. Here's an example of a three-tier lesson structure:

1. **Entry Level:** Represents mastery of the identified standard or standards.
2. **Advanced Level:** Represents a more complex task designed to demonstrate a deeper understanding of the content. In this tier, the student is asked to demonstrate application of the concept through the task provided.
3. **Challenge Level:** The most advanced level; in this tier, students demonstrate the ability to analyze, synthesize, and evaluate the content presented.

When developing a tiered lesson, remember that changes to the various levels can be incremental. Small changes in complexity have a significant impact on the challenge level of the task. Simply making a task harder is not the goal; harder tasks tire the brain, but increasing complexity is brain-engaging. Consider how Ms. Reynolds uses tiered lessons in her primary classroom in the following scenario.

Classroom Scenario

In Ms. Reynolds's first-grade cluster classroom, students have been learning about polar animals. Based on her diagnostic preassessment data, she knows that her learners are at a variety of levels. The standards that she wishes to address require the student to identify and represent various elements related to the life of the polar animal. To maintain the appropriate level of engagement, Ms. Reynolds decides to use a tiered lesson format.

Figure 6.1 Tiered Lesson Example

Level 1: Mastery. Listen to the polar animal book selected by Ms. Reynolds at the listening center. Choose a poster worksheet and complete it.

Level 2: Application Mastery. Select and read a polar animal book. Create a poster showing at least four of the categories we have studied.

Level 3: Advanced. Select and read two polar animal books. Contrast and compare information about the animals' habitats, food, life cycles, and one other element of your choice. Create a poster to share your information.

By allowing her students to work at varied levels of complexity, Ms. Reynolds seeks to ensure that all learners are appropriately engaged in their learning. The content to be addressed remains the same, or similar, but the task complexity has been adjusted to foster engagement.

THINKING TRIANGLES

The thinking triangle promotes the organization of information and can serve to move students into the summarization process. Students can be assessed on accuracy of information and depth and complexity of content understanding. You can adapt the triangles for use with primary source analysis and primary image analysis. Working in groups using primary source documents or images, students can demonstrate their understanding of the content and their ability to articulate that understanding in a succinct manner. This activity can be used at the beginning of a unit to get a sense of student background knowledge, attitudes, and thinking processes, or at any point in the unit to assess student ability to make connections and demonstrate new understandings. To develop a thinking triangle, students begin a succinct word retrieval process that encourages the development of an extensive vocabulary. This process supports both the advanced students who need to refine and hone their vocabulary and the ELL students for whom vocabulary development can be a challenge. The structured approach offers both groups of learners a venue for expression. **Figure 6.2** shows an example thinking triangle for the accompanying language arts scenario.

Classroom Scenario

Pretesting and classroom observations allow Mr. Warren to group his fifth-grade language arts learners for the upcoming poetry unit. Imagery is the starting point for the unit and his learners vary in their vocabulary development and ability to represent their thoughts using poetic imagery. He decides to use learning teams and groups students based on their understandings of imagery. Each group creates poems within thinking triangles to demonstrate their understandings of the topic. See figure 6.2.

Figure 6.2 Thinking Triangle: Poetry Example[1]

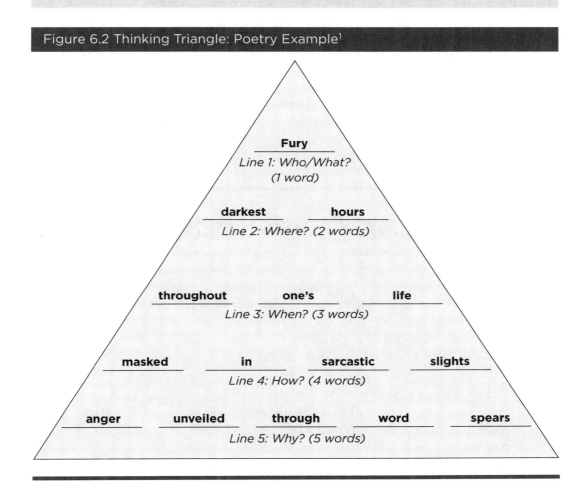

"I AM'S"

"I Am's" personally connect the learner to the topic of study. This strategy fosters vocabulary development, analysis of content, and use of point of view in the writing process. The strategy promotes the application of inference skills and conceptual thinking. Providing varied sentence starters can easily increase complexity and rigor to match student capabilities. See **figure 6.3** for an example from a social studies lesson on the United States Constitution. The underlined words were filled in by a student.

1. Kingore, B. (2008). *Teaching Without Nonsense: Translating Research Into Effective Practice*. Austin, TX: Professional Associates Publishing. Used with permission.

> **Figure 6.3 "I Am": Social Studies Example[2]**
>
> I am <u>yesterday</u>, <u>today</u>, and <u>tomorrow</u>.
>
> I appreciate <u>justice</u> but not <u>necessarily fairness</u>.
>
> <u>Equality</u>, <u>liberty</u>, and <u>perseverance</u> are important to me.
>
> I think <u>I am clear</u>, but <u>I am often misinterpreted</u>.
>
> I wonder if <u>my concepts are valued today</u>.
>
> I care about <u>the past</u> and <u>the future</u>.
>
> I can <u>settle disputes</u> and <u>establish precedents</u>.
>
> I want <u>to be valued</u>.
>
> The <u>future of my existence</u> is often questioned.
>
> So, I <u>seek men with both vision to the future and a value of the past</u>.
>
> This is who I am! I am <u>the United States Constitution</u>.
>
> I am <u>foundational</u> (synonym or metaphor).

CHOICE BOARDS/EXTENSION MENUS

A choice board is a graphic organizer that lets students choose how they will learn a concept. A typical board has nine squares, however, there is no minimum or maximum. Inside each square is an activity. Students can choose one or several activities to complete. Choice boards can be organized so students need to finish one square before moving on to the next, or they can be organized randomly. The level of difficulty of the activities can vary or stay consistent. In most cases, choice boards revolve around a single concept or learning expectation you want the student to focus on. The activities can be structured around Gardner's multiple intelligences, Bloom's taxonomy, a specific interest of a student or group of students, or DOK (depth of knowledge) levels. A choice board could be for a single lesson, a weeklong lesson, or even a monthlong period of study. To create a choice board:

- Identify the most important elements of a lesson or unit.
- Create a required assignment or project that reflects the minimum understanding you expect all students to achieve.
- Create negotiables that expand upon the minimum understandings. Negotiables are those items that the teacher is willing to discuss and adjust with the student. It may be a format, a due date, or any other item the teacher is willing to negotiate on. Negotiables give students a feeling of deeper ownership of the activity. They often require students to go beyond the basic levels of Bloom's taxonomy and/or extend into levels 3 and 4 of Webb's DOK.

The most recognized structure for choice boards and extension activities is the traditional three-by-three grid. Extension lessons come in all different shapes and sizes, but each one offers students choices in how they demonstrate understanding. Extension lessons can also give students a relevant, go-to assignment when they have independent time. Provide an extension menu for students who have compacted

---

2. Kingore, B. (2008). *Teaching Without Nonsense: Translating Research Into Effective Practice*. Austin, TX: Professional Associates Publishing. Used with permission.

out of a lesson or unit of study. The menu offers students a set of possible assignment options. The number of required tasks is determined by the teacher. In most instances, the tasks are grouped by complexity; each activity offers the learner a different opportunity to further develop understanding and apply knowledge. See **figure 6.4** for an example of a language arts choice board.

Consider creating an extension menu for each major topic you are teaching. Doing so helps students move back and forth between whole-class instruction and extension activities as needed. Create an extension folder for each student in the class. Pretest results can guide you on which levels of activities each student needs. Students can work on extension activities individually, in pairs, or in small groups. Allow for time each week for *all* students to work on their extension lessons. This provides opportunities for struggling students and other diverse learners (who might never compact out of your regular lessons) to also engage in extension activities. Every learner should have the opportunity to engage in the enrichment offered in an extension menu. See page 154 for a reproducible extension menu planning form.

Figure 6.4 Choice Board/Extension Menu: Vocabulary Example		
Vocab Talk 1. Select a word from the week's list. 2. Define the word, state its origin and part of speech, and use it in a sentence. 3. Present the word to the class in a memorable way.	**Use/Misuse Sentences** 1. Write 2 sentences using the assigned word correctly. 2. Write 2 sentences using the word incorrectly. 3. Share your sentences with another group. Did you trick them?	**Four Square** 1. Fold paper into fourths. 2. Roll dice to determine what will go in each box: (1) Definition (2) Sentence (3) Origin (4) Antonym/Synonym (5) Part of Speech (6) Illustration
Wordy Story Rewrite the wordy story in your text using everyday language instead of vocab words. Or, create your own wordy story and have another team rewrite it.	**Rewrite** Choose one or two "rewrites" from the book and rewrite the sentences using synonyms.	**Strip It** 1. Choose 2 words. 2. Create a 4-frame comic strip using the 2 words. 3. Give it a title and details.
Figurative Language Sentences ▪ Write 3 alliterative sentences using your words. ▪ Write 3 imagery/sensory sentences using them. ▪ Write 3 rhyming sentences using them.	**Sell a Word** Choose a word and sell it using a propaganda strategy: ▪ Peer pressure ▪ Bandwagon ▪ Repetition ▪ Testimonial ▪ Transfer ▪ Emotional/loaded words	**Design a Review Game** With your team, create a review game for the class to play. Active engagement by all is required.

"MAKE 10" BOARDS

In this strategy, each activity in a choice board is given a point value. The value denotes the level of complexity and effort the task will require. Students must select different activities that add to a total of ten or more points. For example, one student might choose an eight-point and a two-point activity, while another might select two five-point activities. When students can choose their own learning activities, their engagement is dramatically increased.

Figure 6.5 "Make 10" Board: Social Studies Example			
ANCIENT CHINA "MAKE 10" BOARD			
Select a key item in the Chinese Celebration of the New Year and create it. Be prepared to share its significance with the class. **Point Value 1**	Research the Great Wall of China. Create a PowerPoint or Prezi to share your research. Be sure to include pictures and cite your resources. **Point Value 3**	Design a colorful map of Ancient China. Include 3 major rivers, mountain ranges, deserts, major cities, and the location of the Great Wall. Label elements and tell their significance to the Chinese culture. **Point Value 5**	An emperor ruled each of the Chinese dynasties. Select a dynasty and develop 8 to 10 interview questions you would ask him. Provide the answers you'd expect based on your research. **Point Value 2**
"Three Doctrines" or "Three Teachings"—Confucianism, Taoism, and Buddhism—played a key role in daily life. Create a graphic to show the relationships within these teachings. **Point Value 5**	Design a cookbook to represent the choices of various regions during the period in Chinese history. Include illustrations and possible menu options. (10-page minimum) **Point Value 6**	In a team, complete the Webquest listed below. Include all components of the quest. zunal.com/ webquest. php?w=211452 **Point Value 8**	Make a pop-up book of the animals depicted on the Chinese calendar. Include information about the character and significance of each. Must have color, text, and one pop-up per page. (6-page minimum) **Point Value 5**
Make a tree map for the 5 dynasties. Provide 5 key facts for each dynasty along with an illustration that represents the dynasty. **Point Value 2**	Select a Chinese proverb. Create a trifold brochure that depicts the proverb, its meaning, and a proverb of your own that teaches the same life lesson. (Keep in mind the 3 Cs: creativity, color, and clarity.) **Point Value 5**	Research the Silk Route. Create a collage depicting its significance. Include: 1) Plants and Food 2) Tech/Inventions: from China to the West 3) Tech/Inventions: from the West to China 4) Religion 5) Population **Point Value 3**	Create a crossword using a minimum of 20 vocabulary words from the unit on Ancient China. Provide a key. **Point Value 1**

RESTAURANT MENUS

A lesson extension can also be presented in a restaurant menu format, letting students make decisions about how they will meet lesson requirements. A menu could be made for a single lesson, a weeklong lesson, or even a monthlong period of study. Once you have decided on the essential understandings and skills, you can begin to create the menu.

Steps for creating a restaurant menu of learning choices:

1. Identify the most important elements of a lesson or unit.

2. Create a "must do" or required assignment or project that reflects the mastery-level understanding you expect all students to achieve. This is the "main dish" on the menu. It should be at a DOK level 2 or 3 to ensure that students can not only recall the knowledge gained but also put it to use in a meaningful manner.

3. Design negotiables that expand upon the main dish or "must do" assignment or project. These activities are the "appetizers" and "side dishes" on the menu. They often require students to go beyond DOK levels 1 and 2; they offer more strategic and extended thinking options. For example, they include activities that require synthesis, analysis, or evaluation.

4. Design optional assignments or projects that are high-interest and provide enrichment. These are the "desserts" on the menu.

Figure 6.6 Restaurant Menu Template[3]

Appetizers (Negotiables)
- A list of assignments or projects
- Students select one item to complete

The Main Dish (Imperatives)
- An assignment or project that everyone must complete

Side Dishes (Negotiables)
- A list of assignments or projects
- Students select two items to complete

Desserts (Options)
- Optional but irresistible assignments or projects
- Options should be high-interest and challenging
- Students choose one of these enrichment options

Classroom Scenario

Second-grade teacher Miss Martin believes that this grade level is a great place to start the extension menu process. In her class, each student is given a "weekly allowance" that they can spend toward ordering activities off the "menu." Students may not exceed their account balance. In this way, Miss Martin differentiates the activities available to different learners at multiple levels. Students need to make decisions based on several variables, such as choosing food in different categories (which represent different levels and learning preferences) while also monitoring their spending.

---

3. Wormeli, R. (2005). *Fair Isn't Always Equal: Assessing & Grading in the Differentiated Classroom.* Portland, ME: Stenhouse Publishers, 62–65.

Figure 6.7 Restaurant Menu Example

CAFÉ TIME

When you have completed your assigned task, it is Café Time. Choose 1 appetizer, 1 entrée, and 1 dessert. Be sure to check your account balance to know how much money you have to spend. Take your time, a meal is to be savored!

APPETIZERS

Design Plate	Using the math cubes, design and solve 6 different math problems.	$4
Musical Medley	Create a song about one of the weather storms we are studying. You will perform it tomorrow after lunch.	$7
Build Blocks	Using the tangrams, create one of the designs provided. Did you use all of the tangrams?	$5

ENTRÉES

Letter Salad	Pour 10 to 15 letter blocks into a bowl. Create as many new words as you can using the blocks.	$9
Mail Munch	Grab a postcard from the mail center. Choose a character from our current story. Send a postcard from the character (3 sentence minimum). Create a color illustration for your card.	$10
Puzzle Power	Create a Puzzle Power picture that relates to the weekly topic. Cut up your puzzle and share it with a friend.	$14

DESSERT

Sundae Builder	Using the Sundae Fraction cards, build a sundae that totals one whole.	$6
Game Player	Design a math card game for two or more players. Be sure to write your rules on the Rule Card.	$8

Developing Creative Thinking: Fluency, Flexibility, Elaboration, and Originality

Following is a simple, yet effective way to differentiate daily by developing creative thinking in your students while working in any grouping structure. This method requires little to no advanced preparation and can engage and challenge students at all levels of learning.

Paul Torrance, best known for his Torrance Tests of Creative Thinking, disrupted long-held beliefs in the 1960s about intelligence as the predictor of success. His creative thinking test created a mind shift and opened the door for new understandings about creativity that could be enhanced through instruction and practice.[4] One method for developing creative thinking that emerged from Torrance's work is the

---

4. Torrance, E. P. (1979). *The Search for Satori and Creativity.* Buffalo, NY: Creative Education Foundation.

process of fluency, flexibility, elaboration, and originality. The process has a group of students brainstorm and generate a bank of ideas, then examine those ideas from varying perspectives. Students then hone in on one or more idea to elaborate upon, which can lead them to develop original ideas.

Fluency. The ability to quickly generate a large quantity of diverse ideas and/or solutions to problems. Brainstorming activities promote fluency of ideas.

Ask students:

- How many _____?
- What kinds of _____?
- What else _____?

Flexibility. The ability to look at things from different perspectives; to pursue different angles of thinking; and to make remote associations. Flexible thinking extends fluency. It helps students generate and promote responses that deviate from typical thought patterns.

Ask students:

- Can you think of a different way to _____?
- What else might be happening?
- What other things are possible?

Elaboration. The ability to add to an idea; to give details, build groups of associated ideas, and expand on ideas to develop complex thoughts. Elaboration requires students to ask more questions and seek more answers than are generally given; it encourages focusing on solutions and developing ideas further.

Ask students:

- What can you add to make this idea more interesting/complete?
- What else can you tell me about _____?
- Using these guidelines, what can you develop?
- Using these basic elements, what can you create?

Originality. The ability to produce clever, unique, unusual responses. The more ideas that are produced (fluency), the higher the chance that original ideas will emerge. The goal is that some students will produce original ideas as a result of thinking differently during flexibility exercises.

Ask students:

- How could you make it different?
- How can you change _____ to make _____?
- How can you combine _____ and _____ to make something new?

You can see the level of complexity increase with the questioning at each level.

Classroom Scenario

Mrs. Brown asks her students to think about how Charlotte changes in *True Confessions of Charlotte Doyle*. She tells her students, "Picture Charlotte walking up the ramp of the ship. How is she feeling? Describe her in one word." One by one students call out words that describe Charlotte at that time, while one student records the descriptive words (fluency). Students form groups of four to five students. Students in each group select words from the word bank and discuss how the words described Charlotte at a specific time in the story (flexibility). Mrs. Brown distributes a large, blank, white puzzle piece to each group. Each group then has a discussion elaborating on their selected words until a picture emerges (elaboration). Students depict Charlotte changing through images that emerge from their discussions (originality). Mrs. Brown then puts the puzzle pieces together to show the ways the students saw Charlotte develop and change throughout the story.

In Closing

In this chapter, we described several methods for differentiating daily in mixed-ability classes. We began by emphasizing the importance of using diagnostic and formative assessments to compact curriculum. We then introduced several lesson extensions to use for those students who compact out of the regular curriculum. Lesson extensions offer a myriad of means through which content can be addressed by the learner. Choice is often a key feature of a lesson extension; it empowers learners. Tiered lessons provide varied entry points for the learner, thus ensuring that task complexity and instruction are tailored to the learner's readiness level. All these differentiation tools meet student needs and rely on diagnostic and formative assessment to determine where the learner resides along the learning continuum of the standards.

Tiered Lesson Planning Chart

Unit: _____

REQUIRED STANDARD	ENTRY-LEVEL ACTIVITIES	ADVANCED ACTIVITIES	MOST CHALLENGING ACTIVITIES

Adapted from *The Cluster Grouping Handbook: A Schoolwide Model: How to Challenge Gifted Students and Improve Achievement for All* by Susan Winebrenner and Dina Brulles, Free Spirit Publishing, 2008. Used with permission.

Extension Menu Planning Form

Step One: Key questions to be answered.
- What standards will you address?

- How long will students have to work on the extension?

- Is this extension for all students or for a specific group of learners?

- What format will be used?
  - ❏ 3 x 3 grid
  - ❏ List of options
  - ❏ Restaurant menu
  - ❏ Other framework _____
  - ❏ How will you assess the lesson extension activities?

Step Two: Design your activities to incorporate Bloom's taxonomy or Webb's depth of knowledge levels. This helps ensure that your options provide learning opportunities at varied levels of complexity.

Step Three: What learning styles have you addressed?

Standards: _____

For whom: _____   Time frame: _____

Format: _____   Assessment: _____

Extension Lesson Activities

1.

2.

3.

4.

5.

6.

7.

8.

9. Open Option: Teacher Approval Required

CHAPTER 7
Differentiating Digitally in Groups

GUIDING QUESTIONS
- How can I support my students in becoming good digital citizens?
- How can I design group learning activities that both differentiate and use technology appropriately and successfully with students?
- How do I and my students evaluate a digital resource to determine if it is valid?

Today's teachers have access to a multitude of resources that open a wealth of learning opportunities for students. Using examples shared with us by teachers from the Paradise Valley Unified School District, we will demonstrate digital tools and apps that can engage and challenge students. We will show how to access these resources and incorporate them into the standard curriculum within various grouping scenarios.

Today's students are digital natives; they do not know a world without advanced technology. Whether you love it or not, technology is here to stay. Teachers with whom we work have embraced technology by embedding opportunities for their students to interact with each other and with technology.

In this chapter, we describe technology-based group lessons our teachers have developed and implemented. You will see how teachers are learning along with their students, even if this means stepping outside of their comfort zones. We are all learning together as we integrate innovative technologies into twenty-first century classrooms. You will see that when technology is embedded into the learning environment, differentiation happens naturally.

Grouping and Collaborating in a Digital World

The digital age has brought about a revolution in the classroom. No longer is it the norm to learn from textbooks and chalkboards; rather, students are digitally connecting to resources and to other students within their school and around the world. Technology has opened up a world of learning and opportunity that did not exist a mere decade ago.

These new digital learning opportunities encourage students to collaborate in numerous ways and in any grouping structure. Students of all ability levels and interests can learn and work collaboratively in groups in different locations. Some examples include groups of students collaborating digitally:
- Within the same class
- Within the same school

- Within the same district
- Across the nation
- Internationally

Although the digital world offers amazing grouping and learning opportunities for students, it also presents new challenges for teachers and students. The use of digital and social media has highlighted bullying, personal security, and privacy concerns. Teaching students digital etiquette and how to manage their online reputations have become necessary parts of the instructional repertoire as a teacher. Common Sense Media shares eight elements of digital citizenship that should find their way into today's classrooms.[1] These elements are:

- internet safety
- privacy and security
- relationships and communication
- cyberbullying
- digital footprint and reputation
- self-image and identity
- information literacy
- creative credit and copyright

When taught explicitly, these eight elements help your students safely and successfully navigate the technological world in which they live. With the ever-evolving mindset on student collaboration in a digital world comes new instructional considerations, methods, and tools for teachers and students.

The Padagogy Wheel: Integrate Apps with Purpose

When integrating technology into instruction, a key question becomes: is the technology supporting and enhancing the pedagogy? The Padagogy Wheel, created by Allan Carrington, is a tool that helps you place sound teaching methods at the center of instruction when using digital resources.[2] The Padagogy Wheel gives teachers an at-hand reference that ties apps to specific learning outcomes directly connected to modern pedagogies and theories. Your pedagogy should determine the apps you select to use in the classroom, not the other way around. Making connections among the learning objectives, student development and motivation, and an app's features provides an optimal learning opportunity. Connecting groups of students with the appropriate digital application links learners in a way that both motivates and engages. Access the Padagogy Wheel at designingoutcomes.com/english-speaking-world-v5-0 to help you develop lesson plans, curriculum plans, learning centers, and much more.

The Padagogy Wheel promotes student-driven learning at all levels, which increases motivation and engagement. As discussed in chapter 5, students thrive in

---

1. Common Sense Education. (n.d.) "Digital Citizenship." Accessed Nov. 22, 2017, at commonsense.org/education/digital-citizenship.
2. Padagogy Wheel V5 developed by Allan Carrington. Designing Outcomes, Adelaide, Australia. designingoutcomes.com/english-speaking-world-v5-0

project-based learning experiences where they can integrate aspects of their previous learning. The wheel enables you to focus those efforts using suggested tools and methods for integrating appropriate technology to support pedagogy. It draws upon the digital capabilities of today's learners and their motivation to engage with digital formats. When we mesh technology and critical thinking, the result for students is often a highly motivating learning experience. You might struggle to find a way to integrate technology with the demands of curriculum and student learning needs. Looking at the pieces of the wheel—the apps, learning goals, and cognitive actions— and how they work in unison will aid you in this integration.

To get the most out of the Padagogy Wheel, use it as a series of prompts or interconnected gears to inform your teaching, from planning to implementation. Tobias Rodemerk from the State Institute for School Development Baden-Württemberg (LS), Germany, encourages us to think of the wheel in a gear framework:

The Attributes Gear. This is the core of learning design. At this gear in the center of the wheel, one you constantly revisit, are things like ethics, responsibility, and citizenship. Ask yourself the question, "What makes the learner successful?" How does everything I do support these attributes and capabilities needed for success?

The Motivation Gear. This gear, the second ring of the wheel, focuses on developing learner autonomy, mastery, and purpose.

The Bloom's Gear. The third, fourth, and fifth rings in the wheel promote the design of learning objectives that achieve higher-order thinking. Try to create at least one learning objective for each category.

The Technology Gear. It is important to ask, "How can this serve my pedagogy?" Using technology, whether in app or website form, simply to say that the lesson has a technology component is not a reason to use it. The apps noted in the sixth ring of the wheel are only suggestions; they may lead you to look for better ones and combine more than one in a learning sequence.

The SAMR Model (Substitution/Augmentation/Modification/ Redefinition) Gear. It is at this gear, the outer ring of the wheel, that you must determine how the technologies chosen will be implemented within the learning environment.

If you take a slice from the Padagogy Wheel, you can see how the structures come into play. One might start at the analyze portion of the Bloom's Gear, as with the following example.

Classroom Scenario

After reading *The Secret Garden*, students are to select one of the two protagonists, Mary or Colin. Both characters change significantly over the course of the novel. Students select three specific character traits evidenced by their chosen protagonist. Comparing and contrasting behaviors of the character as the novel evolves, students develop a representation depicting the growth of the character.

The next step is to determine the technology choice or choices that will provide the best connection to the task. In this case, Popplet is the app of choice.

Popplet is a tool used by many educators due to its flexibility. It connects with learners at varied grade levels and is perfect for reading both fiction and nonfiction. When using this resource, students can create a graphic organizer in a bubble format. They can include graphics, titles, and text to explain and detail their information. Students agree that this is an easy-to-use site to display a significant amount of relevant information to meet their objectives. The tool can be used with a small group or individually.

Differentiating with Bloom's Digital Taxonomy

Bloom's Digital Taxonomy offers yet another way of looking at digital tools and their integration with student learning (see **figure 7.1**). The taxonomy helps you navigate through the many resources available in today's digital classroom. Activities can be tailored to address the experience and knowledge level of the student thus generating an appropriately challenging and engaging learning opportunity.

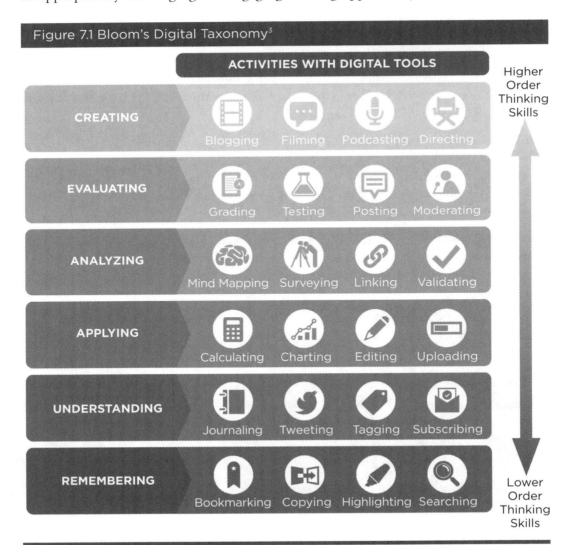

Figure 7.1 Bloom's Digital Taxonomy[3]

ACTIVITIES WITH DIGITAL TOOLS

Higher Order Thinking Skills

CREATING — Blogging, Filming, Podcasting, Directing

EVALUATING — Grading, Testing, Posting, Moderating

ANALYZING — Mind Mapping, Surveying, Linking, Validating

APPLYING — Calculating, Charting, Editing, Uploading

UNDERSTANDING — Journaling, Tweeting, Tagging, Subscribing

REMEMBERING — Bookmarking, Copying, Highlighting, Searching

Lower Order Thinking Skills

3. Image by Ron Carranza. Used with permission.

Each level within the digital taxonomy lends itself to specific activities students can use with different digital tools. The following list describes the types of activities that support learning in each of these levels.[4] When students work in small, flexible groups, their specific area of study can be supported using these varied tools.

Remembering. Recalling facts and basic concepts or retrieving material. *Use digital tools for:* bookmarking, copying, googling, bullet-pointing, highlighting, group networking, and searching.

Understanding. Explaining ideas and concepts or constructing meaning from written material or graphics. *Use digital tools for:* advanced searching, annotating, blog journaling, tweeting, tagging, commenting, and subscribing.

Applying. Using information in new situations such as models, diagrams, or presentations. *Use digital tools for:* calculating, charting, editing, presenting, uploading, operating, and sharing with a group.

Analyzing. Drawing connections among ideas and concepts or determining how each part interrelates to an overall structure or purpose. *Use digital tools for:* mashing, mind-mapping, surveying, linking, and validating sources.

Evaluating. Justifying a stand or decision; making judgments based on criteria and standards through checking and critiquing. *Use digital tools for:* grading, networking, rating, testing, reflecting, reviewing, blog commenting, posting, and moderating.

Creating. Producing new or original work. *Use digital tools for:* animating, blogging, filming, podcasting, publishing, simulating, wiki building, video blogging, programming, and directing.

Classroom Scenario

Mrs. Rincon groups her students based on their knowledge of the events leading up to the Boston Tea Party. Once grouped, she decides that Bloom's digital taxonomy would be an engaging way to level the activities for her students.

At the understanding level, Mrs. Rincon asks seven of the students, including her two special needs students, to respond to prompts she provides in a digital journal. Students use their textbook and other digital resources to gather the information needed. In addition to gathering printed source information, students will search for images that represent the information. Images and text will be input into the digital journal.

A second group of students, including three ELL students, working at the analysis level are asked to use their understandings by analyzing the information to construct a mind map and create a foldable to share the information. Students may select the foldable of their choice from the set taught previously to the class or create an original of their own.

Mrs. Rincon's advanced learners are given the option of creating a podcast or a video to share their understandings. Students are required not only to

---

4. Adapted from "Integrating Technology with Bloom's Taxonomy," by Obiageli Sneed (May 9, 2016). teachonline.asu.edu/2016/05/integrating-technology-blooms-taxonomy.

present the facts but also to provide an analysis of the event as it related to the onset of the war.

By grouping her students and utilizing the digital taxonomy, Mrs. Rincon seeks to ensure that students are provided with activities that offer the appropriate level of challenge.

Integrating Technology in Group Work

In this technology-rich world, it is vital that educational methods and strategies keep pace if we hope to engage the learners that enter our classrooms. This section details some popular apps and programs currently being used by teachers to differentiate instruction and optimize flexible grouping.

APPS TO AID SMALL-GROUP LEARNING

What could happen if technology enabled you to transform a small-group task from a written format to a visual one? The answer is simple: engagement, rigor, and challenge could occur. Using innovative learning tools benefits all learners, as is shown in the following classroom scenarios.

Classroom Scenario

Mrs. Cutler has her students use free apps to demonstrate support with textual evidence, a standard in classrooms across the nation. She groups her students in teams based on their level of proficiency with the text and ability to identify character traits in *Elizabeth I* by Milton Meltzer. The next step is for each group to find textual evidence that supports the traits they identified and, finally, to create a visual representation. Using a photo collage app, teams represent the character as well as the mood/theme of the literature. Teams share their collages; other teams try to identify which character traits and the mood/theme each team is striving to represent.[5]

Vocabulary takes on a new dimension when technology is added to the mix. Photo collage apps such as **Pic Collage** offer many options for learners. Students create a collage to show a pictorial representation of the meaning of a word, a great tool for visual learners and those not fluent in English. Teaming your visual learners with those who do not see learning through this lens is a great way to support both groups. Students with strong nonverbal skills often excel in this format, since it provides them an outlet to use abstract visual reasoning skills to represent ideas instead of the traditional written format.

The **Trading Card** app also offers a way for students to demonstrate their understanding related to characterization and vocabulary. This app is great for first-time users because it supplies guiding questions to assist students in the development and design process. The final product is a trading card much like the ones used by major league athletes.

---

5. Randi Posner Cutler is the gifted specialist at Desert Springs Elementary School in the Paradise Valley Unified School District, Arizona. Example used with permission.

Classroom Scenario

Technology can also be used to assess the depth of student understanding. Mrs. Warner's student groups use technology as they learn to participate in a Socratic seminar. First, they need to understand the difference between a dialogue and a debate. Rather than ask students to define the terms, Mrs. Warner knows technology will help them go one step further. Once students determine the meanings of *dialogue* and *debate*, they break into groups to create products that illustrate the difference between the two. Students chose from Pic Collage, **Kahoot!**, or **Popplet** to demonstrate the meaning through a visual representation, a quiz, or even a mind map.

Next, using **iMovie**, groups of students create an island/land of dialogue and an island/land of debate. Next, students design and create an advertisement for the islands in iMovie Trailer format. Students are regrouped and asked to create an original skit that shows examples of dialogue and debate within a short story. The skit is filmed and put into an iMovie presentation.[6]

Classroom Scenario

You may wonder, "Why group and regroup throughout the learning process?" In this scenario, students were moving through the concept of Socratic thought and the elements of Socratic seminars. As student understandings grew, their need for different peer connections grew as well. Grouping students in varied structures helps them develop collaboration skills.

Mrs. Stanton's students were investigating the literary element of plot. The class had read *The Westing Game* and kept a "detective log" with the details of the chapter and an icon or symbol to represent each chapter. The assignment was to create a plot map of the book. The details of the assignment with the objective were provided to students.

The students wondered what Mrs. Stanton would assign as their project, though at the end of the lesson introduction she simply stated, "How you get there is up to you." Quizzical looks appeared on students' faces until they realized that they would be creating and designing a project based on their *own* interests.

The project was to be completed individually, but students were encouraged to work with peers to collaborate and extend their ideas. Several chose to complete the project on paper, designing mountains and road maps depicting the journey of events throughout the story. And several students chose to use digital presentation formats such as **Google Slides** and **Prezi**. Differentiation was evident as each student could take the project to their own ability level, depth of knowledge of text, and technological ability. Students established their own groups based on their mode of presentation, and they collaborated and coached each other throughout the project.[7]

---

6. ElizaBeth Warner is the gifted specialist at North Ranch Elementary School in the Paradise Valley Unified School District, Arizona. Example used with permission.
7. Nancy Stanton is the gifted specialist at Pinnacle Peak Elementary School in the Paradise Valley Unified School District, Arizona. Example used with permission.

Classroom Scenario

Dr. Jason McIntosh uses the website **Plickers.com** to build learning groups in his fourth-grade class. Plickers enables him to create a quick pretest that graphically shows the information in an instant. Here are the steps to follow:

First step: Print off the cards from the Plickers website. Each card has a code that you can read and scan from the front of the classroom using a smartphone or tablet.

Next step: Pose a question to students. Students hold up their cards in one of four orientations (right side up, upside down, turned 90 degrees to the left, or turned 90 degrees to the right) to indicate their answer to the question. Scan the room using your smartphone or tablet.

Final step: Allow Plickers to give the results instantly in the form of a graph and individual results by student. Use the results to create tiered groups.

Another tech tool in Dr. McIntosh's repertoire is the website **Livebinders .com**. Livebinders is a site where you can create digital binders of websites, videos, and links pertaining to a topic. These binders become searchable by all online users. You can have students search for a topic they are interested in to facilitate the research process or have them create a binder of their own.

Dr. McIntosh used this site in a unit he created called "Quests and Quandaries." Students went on a quest to become an expert on a topic of their choosing. Once students determined their areas of interest, Dr. McIntosh handpicked quality live binders from the website and gave students the binder identification numbers. Students then typed in the ID numbers and accessed the content. Students examining similar topics worked together.[8]

APPS TO SUPPORT DIVERSE AND SPECIAL NEEDS LEARNERS

Special needs education has especially benefitted from technology integration. Google Docs, for example, offers a speech-to-text option that can be used to support groups of students struggling with written expression. There are also many programs that will allow text to be read to a learner. With the advent of digital resources such as **newsela.com**, you can customize the reading level of text to meet students' needs. This allows all students to be reading about the same topic but with text at their instructional level.

Classroom Scenario

Mrs. Collins was searching for an article on global warming to share with her sixth-grade students in conjunction with their science unit. Her class consists of a wide range of reading abilities, and finding material suitable for all is always a challenge. The website newsela.com proved to be a perfect tool for her. Once

---

she located the article through the search features, she could tailor it to meet the Lexile reading levels of her flexible groups. All students could participate and be part of the class activities and discussions. To further the experience, Mrs. Collins chose to empower her students to use the site themselves to locate materials for their next project.

GROUPING AND COLLABORATING WITH GOOGLE CLASSROOM

Perhaps chief among all digital resources used by teachers today, Google Apps for Education have changed classroom instruction in numerous ways. The apps offer educators and students viable means of integrating technology with the curriculum and learning needs of students. One app that can help teachers manage differentiated learning is called **Google Classroom**. Google Classroom offers teachers and students a new means of communicating as well as a method for developing a learning environment that connects multiple learners. The app is available to schools with a Google Apps for Education domain. Google Classroom is a way to get all your students in one place and enables you to easily group students, assign work, build discussion, and create a place for students to turn in assignments.

Google Classroom helps you:

Share Resources. You can easily share a document, video, or link with your students.

Create a Lesson. More than simply assigning work to students, this format helps you build an assignment. You can include a lesson description and learning activities and attach multiple documents, links, and videos. Google Classroom puts the entire lesson in one place for individual students or for a group of learners.

Make Class Announcements. Post your announcements to individual students, small groups, or the whole class. Unlike a website with one-way communication, students can comment on the announcement.

Go Paperless. Using Google Docs, you no longer need to collect and pass out paper. You can assign students a blank Google Doc or use a template that your students fill out. Google Classroom creates a copy for each student and gives them a "turn in" option when they are finished.

Notify Students Who Need Help. Know immediately who has and has not completed an assignment. Send an email notification providing tips for success and encouraging the student to work on the assignment.

Post Assignment Q&As. When an assignment is posted, the students can comment on it or post questions. This interaction transcends the walls of the classroom; students can ask questions outside of class. When you post the response, it is available to all the students.

Email Feedback. When returning work to students, you can provide a global note to all the students or individually provide feedback. With Google Classroom you can post a note to the assignment and the student can comment back. This feedback system replaces the one-sided margin note, providing a more dynamic experience.

Create Multiple Files for an Assignment. You can assign multiple documents. This means students can create a multistage project and submit all their pieces in one place.

Collect Data. You can link to a Google form or spreadsheet from an announcement and quickly gather data from students.

Share Materials with Multiple Classes. If you teach multiple sections of the same course, Google Classroom will create the assignment in each section.

Use Polling. You can poll or survey students for multiple purposes, such as to collect formative assessment data. You can also use it for collecting information. For example, you can create an assignment to find out which students are attending a school event. If yes, have students write their names on a Google Doc that contains event information and then submit the assignment. Now you have a clear list of which students are attending and which ones are not.

All these features are wonderful, but the most dynamic aspect of Google Classroom is the ability it provides for collaboration and group work. Here are some examples:

Create Classroom Collaboration. When sharing a document, you can choose if the students can view the document or edit it. Creating a document and giving all the students in the class editing access to it means every student can contribute to a class project.

Create a Discussion. A spreadsheet can be used to collect student opinions on a discussion topic. The ability to have multiple tabs allows for multiple discussion questions. Sharing a single Google spreadsheet with student editing access gets everyone on the same page quickly and gives every student a voice in the discussion.

Capture the Middle of the Process. An important shift in the teacher-student relationship is to get away from being an evaluator and focus on being a coach to your students. Google Classroom places all student work into a folder that is easily accessible from your Google Drive. While students are in the middle of working on their assignment, you can go in and insert comments and guide them through the process.

Collaborative Notetaking. Create a Google document and designate some students to be notetakers for the discussion. Students can collaboratively take notes on the document. Those notes are then easily accessible by the other students through an announcement in Google Classroom.

One Student/One Slide (or One Group/One Slide). Set an assignment to be a single Google Slide presentation that the class can edit. Modify the master slide to provide a template for student work when students insert their own slides.

Track Edits to a Collaborative Document. Instead of sharing a Google Doc that anyone can anonymously edit, Google Classroom can give editing access to a specific group of students for a single document.

Classroom Stream. Through the classroom stream feature, students can connect with others in their class and/or group to dialogue and analyze based on questions posed by you or classmates.

Classroom Scenario

Technology teacher Karen Mensing shares how to incorporate this technology in a meaningful and, yes, fun way! In Ms. Mensing's lesson, students combine a few math lessons to learn about money, calculating sums, calculating differences, and data analysis via Google sheets. To kick off this lesson, each student receives a Mystery Money Egg, opens it, and adds up the contents. Once finished with their calculations, students scan the enclosed QR code to see if the total they calculated matches the amount listed on the code. Students quickly discover that none of the QR codes match the totals! So, for the next step, students figure out the difference between the total listed on the QR code and the actual total. At this point, the group work begins as students locate others with the same color egg as theirs and combine the totals. Students work together to add the totals listed on their codes and compute the difference between their combined money totals and the QR codes.

Next, students return to their seats and access their pvLearners accounts.[9] Using Google apps, students create a spreadsheet to detail their egg contents and share the spreadsheet with the teacher and their Mystery Money Egg partner. Students add a page to their spreadsheet with the combined information from both eggs.

Students enjoy the "mystery" aspect of this lesson and can practice basic math skills and combine those skills with higher-level data tracking and analytics. The Mystery Money Eggs incorporate the four Cs: Students communicate, collaborate, and think critically throughout the lesson; the creativity integration comes when creating the spreadsheet, since students can choose fonts, backgrounds, colors, cell sizes, and so forth.

The rubric for this lesson is reviewed at the beginning and throughout the lesson, so students have a clear understanding of the purpose and how they will be graded. Ms. Mensing uses five different egg colors in total, enabling her to have five different learning levels. Her students are unaware that the colors indicate levels of complexity. However, when students ask if they can trade colors, the answer is a definite "Nope!"[10]

Differentiated Digital Lesson Examples

The following seven figures show examples of how several teachers use digital tools to differentiate instruction for groups working at different levels within the same content.

---

9. pvLearners is the Paradise Valley School District's digital collaboration site where students, teachers, and administrators email, video chat, share lessons, collaborate on projects, and access resources.
10. Karen Mensing is the gifted specialist at Paradise Valley Unified School District, Arizona. Example used with permission.

Figure 7.2 Student-Created Math Video Lessons[11]

Grade Levels: 5 and 6

Subject: Math

Common Core State Standards: Number and Operations: Fractions. Use equivalent fractions as a strategy to add and subtract fractions (other math topics can be used)

Applications: Educreations, Khan Academy

Materials: tablets, fraction lessons/study guides

Procedures:

1. Upon completing lessons on and review of fractions (equivalents, simplifying, adding and subtracting, multiplying and dividing) students are paired to develop a lesson to reteach to the class. Each group is given a different topic related to fractions.

2. Before developing their own lessons, each pair watches a similar lesson on Khan Academy.

3. Each group develops one or more slides on Educreations (or a similar app) and then records the lesson. Groups can incorporate photos, video clips, clip art, or drawings to demonstrate their concepts.

4. After recording, reviewing, and receiving feedback, groups can revise to clarify if they wish.

5. Final projects are presented to the class via a projection system.

6. Students observing the lesson are required to take notes to use as a study guide for the upcoming quiz. Students take notes on laptops using shared Google Docs, so they can collaborate and share notes as a whole group or in small groups, as decided by the teacher. If necessary, additional clarifications about the lessons are made by the teacher before the quiz.

Evaluation/Assessment: Students submit their projects to a shared digital portal. The evaluation is based on appropriately demonstrating the procedures of the lesson, showing examples, and so forth, as outlined on the rubric. After some practice, you can also include a student peer evaluation component.

Adaptations: The lesson can be modified for students working individually, in pairs, or in small groups when compacting out of the regular lesson. Pairing heterogeneously may help support students who do not completely understand the lesson or the technology. This process has worked in fourth through sixth grades for all math topics as a review at the end of a unit, and for checking for understanding. It can be differentiated by level, topic, method of presentations, number of students in a group, and so forth.

Reflections: This lesson was extremely successful; my honors students were highly engaged in the process and enthusiastic in their presentations. The students had to use organizational thinking skills in the process of creating a lesson. The development and preparation required to then teach the lesson pushed their thinking into other aspects of the organizational and computational thinking realm. It was a real eye-opener for both me and my students! Students have successfully used this lesson format for a variety of math topics, such as integers, percentages, fractions, decimals, and exponents.

11. Created by Janice Dwosh, instructional specialist, Boulder Creek Elementary. Used with permission.

Figure 7.3 Step Up to Writing with Google Docs[12]

Grade Level: 2 (general education classroom); 2, 3, and 4 (resource room)

Subject: Writing

Common Core State Standards: Writing: Production and Distribution of Writing. Produce clear and coherent writing in which the development and organization are appropriate to task, purpose, and audience.

Procedures: Students receive an assignment via their Google Classroom. The assignment consists of a paragraph they are to read and determine if it is strong and well developed or if further development is needed. Students use their Step Up color coding strategies to support their responses and explain their thinking. The Step Up to Writing strategy offers learners a color coding system to identify paragraph and essay elements.[13]

Based on student conversations, most students felt that the paragraph was a good one. However, completion of the assignment required students to color-code the different paragraph components as follows: green for topic and concluding sentences, yellow for detail sentences, and red for sentences providing elaboration. As students began the color-coding process, it quickly was evident that their thoughts regarding the paragraph were changing. One student was heard saying, "This paragraph is nothing more than a well-written list." Once students had completed their color-coding, they were asked to share their thoughts. The consensus was that the paragraph needed work. It was seriously lacking in elaborative detail.

Students were paired up and asked to add more red components (elaborative details) to the paragraph. The new paragraphs were shared the following class period. This lesson can be extended by having students write their own paragraphs on the topic. Color-coding the paragraph during the editing process helps create a visual image for the learner.

Figure 7.4 "If I See It, I Can Write It"[14]

Grade Levels: 4, 5, and 6 (Honors students)

Subject: Language Arts

Common Core State Standards: Writing: Production and Distribution of Writing. Produce clear and coherent writing in which the development and organization are appropriate to task, purpose, and audience. With guidance and support from peers and adults, develop and strengthen writing as needed by planning, revising, editing, rewriting, or trying a new approach.

Application: Popplet Lite or Popplet

Materials: tablet with Popplet app, a story to summarize, or ideas to organize

Procedures: The teacher assigns a writing project that first requires the creation of a thinking map (or popplet). The map could require a beginning, middle, and end (sequencing); a compare/contrast of characters (double bubble or Venn diagram); a brainstorm of ideas (circle map); or a categorization of ideas (tree map). The students develop the map using drawings, photos, or text. They present their map to the teacher, student groups, or their class depending on the project. This can be the first step of the writing process or the predecessor to a draft and final copy of

continued →

12. Created by Karen Brown, gifted program mentor. Used with permission.
13. Auman, M. (2015). *Step Up to Writing*. Dallas, TX: Voyager Sopris Learning.
14. Created by Janice Dwosh, instructional specialist, Boulder Creek Elementary. Used with permission.

Figure 7.4 "If I See It, I Can Write It",[14] continued

---

written work. Color and visuals add to the variety and depth of this application and provide a creative approach for students.

Evaluation/Assessment: The popplet can be evaluated separately from the final written work or could be used as a formative evaluation before the final product is created. Some areas for evaluation can be the number of details included, order/sequencing of thoughts, variety of ideas, and so on. It should not be the only evaluation in the final piece of written work, but rather a great starting point to see if students' ideas are sufficient to continue with the project or if adjustments in the process are needed.

Adaptations: This app is great for a wide variety of projects and subject areas, such as reading, vocabulary, writing, summarizing steps in science experiments, and social studies (cause and effect). The choices are endless. Special needs students can produce a visual version instead of a written version. Advanced students can be challenged to use higher levels of thinking (synthesis, evaluation).

Figure 7.5 Videophone Collaboration: Make Positive Change[15]

Grade Level: 5

Background: The students' videophone conference was scheduled during a morning class period when all three teachers at the three different schools had their fifth-grade students grouped together based on interests. Some required classwork to be completed prior to the video conference to prepare students for the activity.

Procedures: Mrs. Banwart proposed using a digital slide show presentation entitled "Kids Make a Difference" that provided an overview of examples and suggestions on how to initiate a project to implement positive change in a school or community. The teachers all viewed the presentation with their students. The students were directed to identify something that they would like to see changed. They brainstormed the topic as a class and recorded their responses. Students then formed groups according to their selected topics. Each group was directed to:

1. Devise a plan for addressing their concern.

2. Answer the five Ws: Who, What, When, Why, and How.

3. Prepare a short presentation about their plan.

4. Designate a spokesperson for the group to participate in the video call.

At the time of the presentation, Mrs. Banworth called both schools and got all three classrooms connected and the project was live! To begin, group spokespersons were seated directly in front of the videophone to make introductions. The students were very excited and accomplished sharing their ideas and their plans. The dialogue was on-task and focused.

Reflection: Students were eager to participate and took their responsibilities very seriously as they prepared for the video conference call. Teachers, acting as moderators, facilitated and then stepped back as the students became totally engaged and were the directors of their own learning.

After this initial joint project, the students requested to continue to collaborate with peers from the other schools. We have begun planning a partnering project where the students will devise their own challenge problems and peers from each of the other two schools will attempt to solve them. All students will participate with a small peer group, which will enable students to have more in-depth conversations,

continued →

---

15. Teacher participants: Mia Banwart, instructional specialist, Desert Cove Elementary; Jennifer Haney, instructional specialist, Aire Libre Elementary; Julie Barncastle, instructional specialist, Arrowhead Elementary

Figure 7.5 Videophone Collaboration: Make Positive Change,[15] continued

will offer a platform for academic discussion, and will foster the collaborative idea of global learning.

The instruction in this lesson example is intentionally straightforward. That is, the lesson itself does not require higher-level thinking skills. As the introductory attempt at using the system, the teachers want their students to learn the basic process first. Once students are familiar with the process, the teachers build in lessons with more depth and complexity. Also of importance is knowing that most of the gifted students in these classrooms are current or former English language learners and students whose home language is Spanish. The teachers can build language development into their lessons while engaging students in challenging concepts and interesting projects.

This example involves grouping in several ways:

1. The advanced students at each school are grouped for content replacement. This grouping is based on testing data.

2. The three teachers grouped themselves based on their Title I school status and the assumption that many of their students did not have the same level of technology in their homes as other students in the district.

3. Students within each of the three classes were further grouped together based on shared interests.

4. The students were then grouped together across the three schools to participate in a book talk.

5. Once connections were made based on interests across the schools, students continued to form small groups with whom to collaborate in future endeavors.

Figure 7.6 Videophone Collaboration with Buddy Classes: Arctic Animal Research[16]

Grade Levels: K (self-contained gifted program); 3 and 4 (gifted classes at the three schools)

Background: Kindergarten students were studying the Arctic region in relation to the Arizona State Standards. Each kindergarten student chose an arctic animal to research. The third- and fourth-grade buddy classes also researched the animals and took notes on the animals their kindergarten buddies were researching.

Procedures:

1. Kindergarten students were each partnered with a student in a third- or fourth-grade self-contained gifted class at another site.

2. The kindergarten and older partners introduced themselves to their buddy counterparts via videophone.

3. The younger and older buddies researched arctic animals using online sites, videos, and nonfiction books. Using a shared Google Doc, students took notes answering some specific scientific questions and some open-ended questions about their animals. Information was gathered and contributed by all the students.

4. Via their shared docs, the older students assisted the kindergarten students in writing rough drafts and final copies of their reports. Together, the pairs integrated artistic creativity by drawing or rendering an image of their arctic animal in its natural habitat, including details the students derived from their research.

5. The reports were presented and shared via videophone to all classes. The final kindergarten research was published in a *Student Treasures* class book and shared across multiple schools.

16. Teacher participants: Christy Wagner, Ph.D., and Sue Leichner at North Ranch Elementary; Melissa Jones and Heidi Befort at Desert Trails Elementary; Emily Skelton at Desert Cove Elementary

Figure 7.7 Ignite Presentations[17]

Grade Levels: 6, 7, and 8 (STEM students)

Procedures: Mrs. Mak routinely gives students a menu of options in her computer science class. After students learn the basics of programming—perhaps through an online course from Stanford University or work with Google CS First programming clubs—they work in teams to create a robot. Teams are formed based on the students' choices of menu options. Students choose the level of complexity—from designing dogs that bark to building miniature disco rooms in which a record plays and lights flash.

Students can also tailor a project to their interests. In a module on architecture, some students designed a playground for Egyptian students using Legos, Build with Chrome, or Minecraft. One student opted to re-create the White House using Minecraft.

Presentations: The Ignite presentation format offers another way for Mrs. Mak to differentiate work based on student interests. Student teams each present their projects to the class using the Ignite presentation method.[18] The presenting team has exactly five minutes and twenty slides, which auto-advance every fifteen seconds, to discuss a topic of interest. This activity enables students to share their passion with their peers—be it nanotechnology and its role in medicine, the physics of roller coasters, or the latest advances in virtual reality.

Figure 7.8 Android App Design[19]

Grade Level: 5 (general education students)

Background: A new experience for me this year was teaching application development to Mrs. Zimmermann's fifth-grade class at Tartesso Elementary. Most of her class was with me the year before for approximately sixty hours of an introduction to programming course using the Scratch platform. I was given one hour a week with her class this year to continue programming with them. I decided to use the MIT App Inventor 2 (AI2) as the platform for programming, since it resembles Scratch and many of the ideas and skills learned with Scratch carry over to AI2. Our kindergarten and first-grade classrooms received tablets this year, which allowed for a genuine audience for these projects

Procedures: I split the class into groups of three students, each group forming their own company. Each company was then assigned to a group of either kindergartners or first graders. The fifth-grade companies met with their kindergartner and first-grade clients at three points throughout this project. Once at the beginning to find out what type of app the students would like for their tablets. Again at mid-year to follow up and discuss progress on the app. The last meeting was to show off what they had created. Each week for the first half of the year, we started the class with a quick review of the previous week and then a mini-lesson featuring one component of the AI2 platform.

The students picked their own groups and then divided the work among themselves to meet the deadlines for different parts of the project. In this way, students differentiated the tasks on their own. The students that were good at programming began on the programming part, others who were better at creating the artwork for their projects got started on art. Students who accomplished their tasks early also helped others in need.

continued →

17. Teacher participant: Janice Mak, STEM teacher, Explorer Middle School
18. Ignite Sessions is a presentation format initiated by the International Society of Technology in Education (ISTE). In this format, presenters have five minutes and twenty slides each to inspire attendees.
19. Teacher participant: Joel Wisser, IT teacher, Saddle Mountain Unified School District

Figure 7.8 Android App Design,[19] continued

Reflection: This project would not have been possible without Google Apps for Education (GAFE). All communication between the students and myself took place in Google Classroom. Students used their GAFE accounts to sign in to AI2. All icon artwork was required to be original and most students chose to create it in Google Drawings. Google Hangouts was used to talk with programmers for advice and Q&A sessions. It was a great learning experience for the students and teacher! The apps were finished to varying degrees of operability, but the students learned to work together to bring their vision of their app to life.

In Closing

In this chapter, we shared many technology-infused teaching and grouping strategies and lessons from the teachers in our district. As you've seen, students of all abilities enjoy the challenge and engagement that occurs in the engaging, collaborative interactions described here. When we let students direct their own learning, especially while using technology, they develop their creativity and build self-reflection skills. Our role as teachers is to facilitate and guide our students in seeking these kinds of innovative learning opportunities.

Conclusion

Our goal in writing this book has been to help educators recognize the purpose and need for forming flexible learning groups. No single grouping structure works ideally for all students all the time, hence the name "flexible" grouping. We flexibly group students to provide a fluid learning environment wherein all students can work at their challenge levels all day, every day, in all content areas. Grouping methods introduced here are intended for students of all abilities and learning needs.

Throughout the book, we've encouraged flexibility not only in grouping methods but also in instructional methods. Students have different learning needs at different times and in different content areas. We demonstrated ways to continually respond to these developing needs as students evolve and progress in their learning.

Of course, grouping students purposefully for instruction is just the first step. Using diagnostic testing to form flexible learning groups sets the stage for effective instruction to occur. To help you support the differentiated learning involved in flexible grouping, we've shared numerous strategies for tiering instruction for the various groups, methods for documenting progress, and strategies to help you manage instruction within these structures.

When we are asked why teachers should group students for instruction, the answer is apparent: to better meet the learning needs of all students. Thank you for joining us on this ambitious journey!

References and Resources

Allan, S. D. (1991). "Ability Grouping Research Reviews: What Do They Say About Grouping and the Gifted?" *Educational Leadership*, 48(6), 60–65.

Anderson, L. W., and Krathwohl, D. R. (2001). *A Taxonomy for Learning, Teaching, and Assessing: A Revision of Bloom's Taxonomy of Educational Objectives.* New York: Longman.

Auman, M. (2015). *Step Up to Writing.* Dallas, TX: Voyager Sopris Learning.

Bray, B., and McClaskey, K. (2015). *Make Learning Personal: The What, Who, WOW, Where, and Why.* Thousand Oaks, CA: Corwin Press.

Brulles, D., and Brown, K. L. (2013). "Teacher Support Is Just a Click Away! Creating an Interactive Resource Site for Today's Teachers." *Educational Technology*, 53(N4), 25–32.

Brulles, D., Brown, K. L., and Winebrenner, S. (2016). *Differentiated Lessons for Every Learner: Standards-Based Activities and Extensions for Middle School.* Waco, TX: Prufrock Press.

Brulles, D., Peters, S. J., and Saunders, R. (2012). "Schoolwide Mathematics Achievement Within the Gifted Cluster Grouping Model." *Journal of Advanced Academics*, 23(3), 200–216.

Brulles, D., Saunders, R., and Cohn, S. J. (2010). "Improving Performance for Gifted Students in a Cluster Grouping Model." *Journal for the Education of the Gifted*, 34(2), 327–350.

Brulles, D., and Winebrenner, S. (2012). "Clustered for Success." *Educational Leadership: For Each to Excel*, 69(5), 41–45.

Brulles, D., and Winebrenner, S. (2011). "The Schoolwide Cluster Grouping Model Restructuring Gifted Education Services for the 21st Century." *Gifted Child Today*, 34(4), 35–46.

Brulles, D., and Winebrenner, S. (January 2011). "Maximizing Gifted Students' Potential in the 21st Century." American Association of School Administrators, aasa.org.

Carrington, A. (n.d.). "Integrating #EdTech with the Padagogy Wheel (episode 28 of TeachThought Podcast). Accessed Nov. 9, 2017 at teachthought.com/podcast /ep-28-integrating-edtech-with-the-padagogy-wheel.

Cash, R. M. (2017). *Advancing Differentiation: Thinking and Learning for the 21st Century*. Minneapolis, MN: Free Spirit Publishing.

Common Sense Education (n.d.). "Digital Citizenship." Accessed Nov. 22, 2017, at commonsense.org/education/digital-citizenship.

Cuban, L. (June 8, 2010). "The Difference Between 'Complicated' and 'Complex' Matters." larrycuban.wordpress.com/2010/06/08/the-difference-between-complicated-and-complex-matters.

Davis, M. (Dec. 5, 2012). "How Collaborative Learning Leads to Student Success." Edutopia. www.edutopia.org/stw-collaborative-learning-college-prep.

Dodge, J. (2009). *25 Quick Formative Assessments for a Differentiated Classroom*. New York: Scholastic.

Envision Gifted: Differentiation for Gifted & Talented Learners. "Understanding Depth and Complexity." Accessed Nov. 22, 2017 at envisiongifted.com/services/understanding-depth-complexity.

Feldhusen, J. F., and Moon, S. M. (1992). "Grouping Gifted Students: Issues and Concerns." *Gifted Child Quarterly*, 36(2), 63–67.

Fiedler, E. D., Lange, R. E, and Winebrenner, S. (2002). "In Search of Reality: Unraveling the Myths About Tracking, Ability Grouping, and the Gifted." *Roeper Review* 24(3), 108–111.

Gentry, M. (1999). "Promoting Student Achievement and Exemplary Classroom Practices Through Cluster Grouping: A Research-Based Alternative to Heterogeneous Elementary Classrooms." Storrs, CT: University of Connecticut, National Research Center on the Gifted and Talented.

Gentry, M., and Mann, R. L. (2008). *Total School Cluster Grouping & Differentiation: A Comprehensive, Research-Based Plan for Raising Student Achievement and Improving Teacher Practices*. Mansfield Center, CT: Creative Learning Press.

Greenwald, N. (November/December 1998). "Songs the Dinosaurs Sang." *Gifted Child Today*, 21(6).

Heacox, D., and Cash, R. M. (2014). *Differentiation for Gifted Learners: Going Beyond the Basics*. Minneapolis, MN: Free Spirit Publishing.

IDRA. (March 31, 2006). "Six Goals of Educational Equity." idra.org/equity-assistance-center/six-goals-of-education-equity.

Kingore, B. (2004). *Differentiation: Simplified, Realistic, and Effective*. Austin, TX: Professional Associates Publishing.

Kingore, B. (2008). *Teaching Without Nonsense: Translating Research Into Effective Practice.* Austin, TX: Professional Associates Publishing.

Knowles, M. S. (1975). *Self-Directed Learning: A Guide for Learners and Teachers.* New York: Association Press.

Kulik, C. C., and Kulik, J. A. (1982). "Effects of Ability Grouping on Secondary School Students: A Meta-Analysis of Evaluation Findings." *American Educational Research Journal,* 19(3), 415–428.

Kulik, J. A., and Kulik, C. C. (1987). "Effects of Ability Grouping on Student Achievement." *Equity & Excellence in Education,* 23(1-2), 22–30.

Kulik, J. A., and Kulik, C. C. (1992). "Meta-Analytic Findings on Grouping Programs." *Gifted Child Quarterly* 36(2), 73–77.

Mississippi Department of Education. (2009). "Webb's Depth of Knowledge Guide: Career and Technical Education Definitions." www.aps.edu/re/documents/resources/Webbs_DOK_Guide.pdf.

Olszewski-Kubilius, P. (May 20, 2013). "Setting the Record Straight on Ability Grouping." www.edweek.org/tm/articles/2013/05/20/fp_olszewski.html.

Page, E., and Keith, T. (1996). "The Elephant in the Classroom: Ability Grouping and the Gifted." In *Intellectual Talent* edited by C. P. Benbow and D. J. Lubinski (Baltimore, MD: Johns Hopkins University Press).

Paul, R. (July 23, 2007). "Critical Thinking in Every Domain of Knowledge and Belief" keynote address. criticalthinking.org/pages/critical-thinking-in-every-domain-of-knowledge-and-belief/698.

Plucker, J. A., and Peters, S. J. (2016). *Excellence Gaps in Education: Expanding Opportunities for Talented Students.* Cambridge, MA: Harvard Education Press.

Puzio, K., and Colby, G. T. (March 2010). "The Effects of Within-Class Grouping on Reading Achievement: A MetaAnalytic Synthesis." Paper presented at the annual meeting of the Society for Research on Educational Effectiveness (SREE), Washington, DC.

Rogers, K. B. (2002). *Re-Forming Gifted Education: Matching the Program to the Child.* Scottsdale, AZ: Great Potential Press.

Sarnat, M. (Nov. 11, 2011). "The Powerful Fours of Creative Thinking." www.jrimagination.com/blog/2011/11/11/the-powerful-fours-of-creative-thinking.html.

Sattler, J. M. (1992). *Assessment of Children: WISC-III and WPPSI-R Supplement.* La Mesa, CA: Jerome M. Sattler, Publisher, Inc.

Sneed, O. (May 9, 2016). "Integrating Technology with Bloom's Taxonomy." teachonline.asu.edu/2016/05/integrating-technology-blooms-taxonomy.

Stanley, T. (2012). *Project-Based Learning for Gifted Students: A Handbook for the 21st-Century Classroom*. Waco, TX: Prufrock Press.

Thompson, M. C., and Thompson, M. B. (2003). *Caesar's English 2*. Unionville, NY: Royal Fireworks Press.

Tomlinson, C. A. (2014). *The Differentiated Classroom: Responding to the Needs of All Learners*. Alexandria, VA: ASCD.

Tomlinson, C. A. (2004). *Differentiation for Gifted and Talented Students*. Thousand Oaks, CA: Corwin Press.

Torrance, E. P. (1979). *The Search for Satori and Creativity*. Buffalo, NY: Creative Education Foundation.

Webb, J. T., et al. (2007). *A Parent's Guide to Gifted Children*. Scottsdale, AZ: Great Potential Press.

West Virginia Education Information System (n.d.). "Teach 21: Preserving the Past." Accessed Nov. 22, 2017 at wveis.k12.wv.us/teach21/public/project/Guide .cfm?upid=3357&tsele1=4&tsele2=104.

Winebrenner, S., and Brulles, D. (2008). *The Cluster Grouping Handbook: A Schoolwide Model: How to Challenge Gifted Students and Improve Achievement for All*. Minneapolis, MN: Free Spirit Publishing.

Winebrenner, S., and Brulles, D. (2014). *Teaching Gifted Kids in Today's Classroom: Strategies and Techniques Every Teacher Can Use*. Minneapolis, MN: Free Spirit Publishing.

Wormeli, R. (2005). *Fair Isn't Always Equal: Assessing & Grading in the Differentiated Classroom*. Portland, ME: Stenhouse Publishers.

Index

Page numbers in *italics* refer to figures; those in **bold** refer to reproducible pages.

About the Authors

Dina Brulles, Ph.D., is a school administrator and the gifted education director for Arizona's Paradise Valley Unified School District. Recognized for her expertise in creating and supervising schoolwide cluster grouping, she also assists districts throughout the United States in developing gifted education programs and serves on the faculty of the Graduate College of Education at Arizona State University. Prior to becoming an administrator, Dina was an elementary classroom teacher, a bilingual teacher, an ESL teacher, and a gifted-cluster teacher. She is coauthor with Susan Winebrenner of *The Cluster Grouping Handbook* and *Teaching Gifted Kids in Today's Classroom*. She lives in Peoria, Arizona.

Karen Brown, M.A., is the gifted program mentor for Arizona's Paradise Valley Unified School District. She supports administrators, teachers, parents, and students in both academics and social-emotional areas. Karen also teaches and facilitates classes in the gifted education master's program at Arizona State University and consults with districts throughout the country on flexible grouping, inclusion, curriculum mapping, curriculum implementation, differentiation strategies, schoolwide cluster grouping, and depth and complexity. Karen is the co-recipient of the 2013 NAGC Professional Development Award and coauthor with Dina Brulles and Susan Winebrenner of *Differentiated Lessons for Every Learner*. Karen lives in Phoenix, Arizona.

Contact Dina and Karen at **giftededucationconsultants.com**.

Other Great Resources from Free Spirit

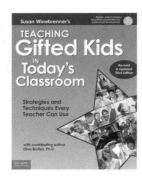

Teaching Gifted Kids in Today's Classroom
Strategies and Techniques Every Teacher Can Use
(Revised & Updated 3rd Edition)
by Susan Winebrenner, M.S., with Dina Brulles, Ph.D.

For teachers and administrators, grades K–12.

256 pp.; paperback; 8½" x 11"; includes digital content

Advancing Differentiation
Thinking and Learning for the 21st Century
(Revised & Updated Edition)
by Richard M. Cash, Ed.D.

For teachers and administrators, grades K–12.

240 pp.; paperback; 8½" x 11"; includes digital content

The Cluster Grouping Handbook: A Schoolwide Model
How to Challenge Gifted Students and Improve Achievement for All
by Susan Winebrenner, M.S., and Dina Brulles, Ph.D.

For teachers and administrators, grades K–8.

224 pp.; paperback; 8½" x 11"; includes digital content

Self-Regulation in the Classroom
Helping Students Learn How to Learn
by Richard M. Cash, Ed.D.

For K–12 teachers, administrators, counselors.

184 pp.; paperback; 8½" x 11"; includes digital content

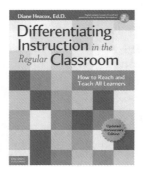

Differentiating Instruction in the Regular Classroom
How to Reach and Teach All Learners
(Updated Anniversary Edition)
by Diane Heacox, Ed.D.

For grades K–12.

176 pp.; paperback; 8½" x 11"; includes digital content

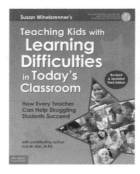

Teaching Kids with Learning Difficulties in Today's Classroom
How Every Teacher Can Help Struggling Students Succeed
(Revised & Updated 3rd Edition)
by Susan Winebrenner, M.S., with Lisa M. Kiss, M.Ed.

For K–12 teachers, administrators, higher education faculty.

288 pp.; paperback; 8½" x 11"; includes digital content

Making Differentiation a Habit
How to Ensure Success in Academically Diverse Classrooms
(Updated Edition)
by Diane Heacox, Ed.D.

For teachers and administrators, grades K–12.

192 pp.; paperback; 8½" x 11"; includes digital content

Many Free Spirit teacher resources include free, downloadable PLC/Book Study Guides. Find them at **freespirit.com/PLC**.

For pricing information, to place an order, or to request a free catalog, contact:

Free Spirit Publishing Inc. • 6325 Sandburg Road, Suite 100 • Minneapolis, MN 55427-3674
toll-free 800.735.7323 • local 612.338.2068 • fax 612.337.5050
help4kids@freespirit.com • www.freespirit.com